Group
Coaching

Group Coaching

A practical guide to optimizing collective talent in any organization

Ro Gorell

KoganPage

LONDON PHILADELPHIA NEW DELHI

First published in Great Britain and the United States in 2013 by Kogan Page Limited

120 Pentonville Road	1518 Walnut Street, Suite 1100	4737/23 Ansari Road
London N1 9JN	Philadelphia PA 19102	Daryaganj
United Kingdom	USA	New Delhi 110002
www.koganpage.com		India

© Ro Gorell, 2013

The right of Ro Gorell to be identified as the author of this work has been asserted by her in accordance with the Copyright, Designs and Patents Act 1988.

ISBN   978 0 7494 6759 3
E-ISBN   978 0 7494 6760 9

British Library Cataloguing-in-Publication Data

A CIP record for this book is available from the British Library.

Library of Congress Cataloging-in-Publication Data

Gorell, Ro.
   Group coaching : a practical guide to optimising collective talent in any organization / Ro Gorell.
– 1st Edition.
      pages cm
   Includes bibliographical references and index.
   ISBN 978-0-7494-6759-3 – ISBN 978-0-7494-6760-9   1. Employees–Coaching of.
2. Organizational change.   I. Title.
   HF5549.5.C53G674 2013
   658.3'124–dc23

                                                                                    2012046364

Typeset by Graphicraft Limited, Hong Kong
Printed and bound in India by Replika Press Pvt Ltd

Dedication

To my husband Ryszard and my mum Dorothy Mee,
who has dedicated her life to helping others.

CONTENTS

PREFACE

Despite the current economic climate, the coaching profession is continuing to emerge and grow year on year. Other forms of development are being squeezed out of company budgets, so isn't it just a little bit curious how coaching seems to be bobbing along, resilient and counter to this general current? As part of this trend, group and team coaching is emerging as the fastest-growing area in this market, both in organizations and for individuals using the internet to coach groups remotely.

I have been coaching for many years and have received some amazing feedback about coaching from clients, for example: 'challenging', 'supportive', 'insightful' and 'inspiring'. Individual coaching can be life changing; imagine what your organization would look like if everyone in it had a 'daily dose' of challenge, inspiration, proactivity and invigoration? It is my contention in this book that this is exactly what group and team coaching can do.

A lot of coaching to date has been concentrated on individual senior executives, and studies have shown that this yields major benefits to the organizations. However, group and team coaching can be made more accessible to a much wider range of people. In addition, by coaching groups and teams together they will learn how to coach each other such that it becomes just the way they work together – a systemic change that benefits everyone.

So much has been written about coaching per se. I have assumed a number of things if you are reading this book either as a coach or as someone looking to introduce coaching into an organization:

- You probably already have a pretty good idea of what coaching is. I am not going to bombard you with elusive or wordy definitions.

- You already know the value that coaching can bring, so I am not going to regurgitate research on validating the benefits that coaching can bring.

- You have a passion for developing talent, and you know what this means and why it is important too.

My experience of reading many books on coaching over the years gave me insight into what strikes a chord and what leaves me cold. I decided that this book would be one from the heart. Yes it will include references and tools, and yes it will be a practical help for coaching groups. What it will also be is free from too much research-based dialectic. It is designed to be accessible with hints for further reading if desired.

However, like a lot of things that just 'happen' in response to a need and are brand-new practices, the whole field of group and team coaching can be a little mystifying and confusing to companies, individuals and coaches alike. In researching the few existing books on group and team coaching I was finding it difficult to get excited about the theories and psychological constructs wrapped around it. I even began to question whether or not I should write the book at all. I found myself asking the question: 'but where is the passion and drive?' Where is the essence of what coaching is really about? And why is any of this important to me or anybody else?

I have endeavoured to connect with you from the words on the page – for me, coaching is a deeply personal connection; I hope that in the following pages you experience a connection with what I have written. I will be exploring key themes on group coaching to encourage your own spirit of exploration in the way you work with groups. I also encourage you to take self-reflection time to challenge your own thinking about what you are doing with groups and what is happening internally for you, to see this as a resource and gift to help you. Essentially I want to challenge established thinking so as to give you, as a group coach, both awareness and choice: the heart of coaching.

So whilst I will offer you some blueprints for effective group and team coaching I will also write in the context of the coach as an adventurer and an experimenter, where the form or structure of an intervention is merely the map you are following that is a guide to point you in the right general direction allowing for diversion along the way. I will share with you my learning about the vulnerabilities that we all feel within group settings to bring some humanity to the process.

In our coaching I hold three tenets dear:

- flexibility;
- purpose;
- being client-centred.

Flexibility

One of my presuppositions for working as a coach – either with a group or one-to-one – is that you are the total resource for your clients. The tools and skills you have are merely one aspect of the resource pool you offer. Being flexible means using these attributes in a way that meets the coachees' needs.

On a group coaching session one of the coachees asked if they could combine two tools to give more depth to the exercise we were doing. The specific tool we were working with was Johari's window. The coachee wanted to expand this to include the use of perceptual positions to give an experiential aspect to the learning.

This was a brilliant example of the coachee using creativity and flexibility to give greater depth to the experience. For me as the group coach there were two things that resonated – that coachees can sometimes feel they need 'permission' to be creative and that as coach it can be easy to fall into the trap of the 'authorized expert'.

Flexibility is about keeping an open mind; this includes how the group might interpret the 'tasks'. It is not for you as the coach to determine how the coachee should interpret meaning; your role is to encourage creativity and flexibility in others to develop resourcefulness and facilitate learning.

Purpose

It is a commonly held belief that real transformation happens when we truly understand our values and beliefs because these motivate behaviour. In coaching terms, transformational coaching is the 'Holy Grail'. It's when you as coach collaborate at a deeper level with your coachees to help them create powerful and meaningful cause for action and change. Uncovering beliefs that limit and values that motivate makes transformation possible.

That's not to say real change can't take place at the task level. This type of change is more focused on a skill or knowledge gap – where the coachees know that they can do something, they just don't have a strategy that works. This is what I call transactional coaching. I'll cover both transformational and transactional coaching in the book.

Transformational coaching in a group setting is where vision and purpose are clear and everyone knows why they're there. It's also an environment in which limiting beliefs are 'declared' so they can be explored. At the beginning of any group coaching session it is really important to find out 'the reason why we are all here'. This is the reason why they've agreed (assuming, of course that they have agreed and not been coerced) to spend x number of hours in a room with other people working together. And the reasons can be many and varied.

The coach should also understand why they're in the room with these people. Are they truly present or are they there just because it's a job? Being truly present is one of the greatest resources any coach can offer a group.

It allows you as the coach to tap into your inner experience and bring this, if relevant, to the group. This leads to my third tenet.

Being client-centred

The coach's role in a coaching relationship is to be client-centred. In other words, you are there for the benefit of the client. We are only human so this has to be a conscious intent – 'Am I doing this for my benefit or the benefit of my client?' 'How does my emotional state help or hinder the client?' Much has been written about the psychodynamic in coaching relationships, and awareness of transference and projection greatly helps the coach decipher what is happening when they experience any emotional response. It's usually the moment your internal dialogue starts to give you messages. Sometimes it's helpful to share, sometimes it isn't. In any event, the truly client-centred coach is aware of and has coping strategies they can call on – it's what I call egoless coaching. These will be different for each coach.

So what is my purpose in writing this book?

One of the key reasons for writing this book is to share my enthusiasm for group coaching as a means to give everyone's talent the chance to shine. I believe that many organizations under-optimize the talent they have. In my book on talent management (Gorell, 2011) I talk about the fact that if you only develop 10 per cent of what is deemed to be the 'top talent' this means that 90 per cent of potential in your organization is left fallow.

Liberating talent – in whatever form – is the purpose behind any coaching collaboration. Coaching groups to help them liberate their talent is something that brings both joy to me as a coach and productivity for organizations. Where group coaching is carried out strategically, ie in the context of a 'bigger picture', the results can be stunning.

My motto and purpose for this book – liberating all talent through group coaching – is what drives me. I base much of the learning on my own experience of coaching and how you can apply this to working with groups and tap into the experiences of those we've coached and other coaches with experience of working with groups. Collaboration is at the heart of group coaching and hopefully this will come to life over the following pages.

Strategic approach to talent management

I've mentioned already that group coaching with strategic intent can lead to improved performance both at an individual and organizational level.

I also pose the question – 'Could group coaching form a strategic approach to talent management?' Back in the 1990s self-directed teams seemed to be the fashion in some organizations. Having experienced this first-hand, the missing ingredient was the facilitator or coach. I would like to offer you a way of integrating group coaching into your talent strategy: a tactic for deploying your talent liberation strategy.

The toolkit

Having now set the scene let's talk about the toolkit. It's important to remember that a tool is just that – an aid to help. Perhaps it's more important to focus on the application of the tool. Some tools work with some groups whereas other groups don't find the same tool as helpful. Receptiveness and readiness are the two words to bear in mind when choosing a group coaching tool. In one group coaching session a relatively simple tool on delegation proved to be a challenge whereas other groups thought the same tool was straightforward and helpful. Quite why such an innocuous tool could provoke such a reaction seemed puzzling – until we started to explore the 'culture'. The context in which you coach groups should never be underestimated and I spend time talking about the 'system' to help give clues as to which tools may help or hinder.

In any event, the tools are there as a guide post for you. How you and the groups you coach use them will be determined by the dynamic and creativity within the group.

Coachees (and coaches) sometimes experience the 'perfection conundrum': they want to do things perfectly and ask – 'Are we doing this right?' Very often the answer 'What does that mean to you?' encourages different perspectives on the 'right way'. Essentially we believe that if the coachees derive value and meaning from the way you use these tools – and there is no harm to them in doing so – you have helped them achieve purpose.

Does that mean you don't need to master the tools?

The responsibility of the coach is facilitation and expertise in working with the tools. After all you are employed for your expertise in group coaching. Confidence and competence enable you as the coach to work flexibly with the tools to help learning. Perfection is not a requirement; mastery is. We will each interpret these tools against our own internal maps. Provided we understand the limitation, application and purpose of the tools and our own limitations as coaches we will be able to develop mastery.

Sometimes it can be helpful to work with a group in a way that encourages mutual discovery. For example, telling the group up front that you haven't worked with a particular tool before and asking their permission to explore together. A word of caution here – ensure the safety of the group by starting with 'safe' topics. It is possible to lurch into areas of the psyche that might make the group feel uncomfortable or vulnerable. Always be aware of your own limitations as a coach.

Coaching conversation style

I have written the book in the style of a coaching conversation and I have endeavoured to coach you through each part of the book. To make the tools accessible and easy to use I have adopted the same style we used in *50 Top Tools For Coaching* as people seem to like this approach. Practice is part of mastery and repetition completes the cycle and I wish you lots of enjoyable, satisfying and purposeful learning experiences working with groups. We are social beings when all is said and done, and optimizing collective talent is a rewarding and meaningful endeavour.

Ro
2013

ACKNOWLEDGEMENTS

We never arrive anywhere 'fully formed' and my thoughts and views are undoubtedly influenced by the books I've read and the many people I've worked and lived with. There are a number of people I wish to single out and say 'thank you' to for their help in making this book come to life. The first person is my husband Ryszard, for tirelessly encouraging me and reading through initial drafts. I am also grateful to my friend Gayl Long, who worked with me on the initial ideas for the book and ignited the spark to carry on. We share a belief that talent is in us all; coaching helps find the key to unlock the treasure. I am grateful to Lorna McDowell, MD of Xenergie, who is an expert in systems coaching, and Angela Dunbar of the Clean Coaching Centre, master clean language and emergent knowledge coach, who practises online group coaching, for their time and insights that I have shared throughout the book. Their insights and experiences no doubt have influenced my thinking and shaped the nature of this book and brought new meaning to the concept 'the whole is greater than [merely] the sum of the parts.' I would also like to say a huge thank you to Kasia Figiel and Martina O'Sullivan, my editors at Kogan Page. Their detailed feedback and suggestions proved invaluable in shaping this book and without their help and encouragement it would have been a very lonely journey. I would also like to acknowledge all the good folks from the Association for Coaching co-coaching forum for allowing me free rein to experiment and push the boundaries of their comfort zones. Those evenings provided me with the first spark of interest in writing this book, and their encouragement and enthusiasm for just 'being' there really made a difference. I am also indebted to Dr Ian May, who trained me in the Deming method when I worked at Siemens. And finally I would like to acknowledge the profound learning experience gifted to me by all my coaching clients, both individuals and groups, since it is from these experiences that I draw my inspiration for this book and retain my fascination with human systems. A heartfelt thank you to you all.

Introduction: taking the group coaching journey

Every organization has hidden talents that are left dormant because too often the focus is on the favoured few; 90 per cent of talent goes untapped. Group Coaching explores the seam of gold waiting to be mined in the organization and provides the means for optimizing collective talents.

Our journey together is in five stages, with each stage building on the previous one, and concludes with exploring how you can liberate talent by integrating group coaching into your organization's talent system. There are some practical tools and tips to help you create your own talent optimization strategy and you'll also get some ideas from others in the field of group coaching. Primarily this book is aimed at coaches who work with organizations – either as internal or as external coaches. If you're not yet using group coaching as a means of optimizing talent then this boPok will help guide you through the areas to consider before you start. Some organizations have been exploring group coaching as a development tool for many years and have not necessarily leveraged the real power of linking it to their talent management strategy because it's buried in the depths of the HR strategy. Linking group coaching with your overall talent system is one of the key ways I explore for optimizing collective talent.

If you don't work with organizations but have your own coaching practice or use coaching as a method for working with clients, the concept of liberating talent will work equally well. The 'organizational' aspect of the group coaching will clearly not be important other than for how the group works together: for example, coaches who use group coaching to work with a collection of different, unrelated coachees. I've seen partnerships form and people start to work collaboratively in such groups even though they are not part of the same organization. In this way, they combine their respective talents and form a virtual organizational link and truly define optimizing collective talents as they form a much wider system.

In researching information for this book I leveraged the collective wisdom of other coaches, in particular two coaches who work in areas that provide specific wisdom on systemic coaching and online coaching. I asked them questions to explore how they help their clients leverage collective talent and during the course of these structured conversations found many similarities and shared philosophies around how we coach our clients. Lorna McDowell specializes in systemic coaching and is the Managing Director of Xenergie, which focuses on organizational transformation coaching and consulting. Much of the work that Lorna and her colleagues specialize in focuses on understanding how groups work together in organizations and helps them gain awareness of the psychodynamics within the system so they are better equipped to increase collective performance and job satisfaction. Angela Dunbar is someone I met many years ago when I first started coaching and is a master clean language and emergent knowledge coach with the Clean Coaching Centre. She also has particular expertise in online group coaching and uses this medium creatively to develop a powerful learning environment in which clients from all over the world can meet in a virtual room irrespective of time zones. The thing that struck me most about her experiences was that a multicultural group provides a richer learning environment simply because of the diverse range of experiences and insights. Throughout the book I have included quotations from these conversations to bring that diversity to life here.

My destination for the book: that you'll take away something practical as well as have a way of tapping into and growing your own latent group coaching potential.

Map of the book so you can navigate your journey

Part One of the book is all about preparing yourself and attaining clarity about purpose, benefits, mindset and approach for group coaching. In Chapter 1, I outline the principal foundation for group coaching – the notion of the egoless coach. Coaching others requires that we coach ourselves first if we are to be congruent and purposeful in our endeavours. In Chapter 2, I explore what the benefits of this approach and group coaching might be for everyone who is part of the coaching process. And in the final chapter of Part One, I outline the importance of understanding the role of coaching and where the boundaries are. The preparation stage is about being totally present with where you, the coachees and the clients are so that you work on firm foundations for the coaching ahead.

In Part Two I tackle the subject of process both from the coaching and group perspective. In Chapter 4 we delve into the notion of process and what specific components are included that make up a process. Flowing on from that I share some of my own blueprints in Chapter 5 to whet your appetite and ignite your own ideas for creating a meaningful group coaching blueprint. And finally we look at the group process and how this impacts and creates energy within the group.

Processes are all well and good but they're meaningless without action and so Part Three looks at how processes become applied through the use of tools and techniques. In Chapter 7 we build on the nature of the group and the dynamics at play by exploring the contracting dynamic within the group setting. Having created a firm basis on which to introduce the coaching sessions, Chapter 8 takes you on a journey of discovery through different tools and their specific uses. Having asked you to think about what tools might be useful for which type of situations I then challenge your creative spark in Chapter 9, where we start to play with different ways of coaching people. There are no right or wrong tools to use – only tools that work – so this chapter is all about getting your ego out of the way and staying client-centred.

No book on coaching would be complete without discussing measurement, and in Part Four I ask you to suspend judgement to explore different perspectives on measurement that better serve the optimization of talent. In Chapter 10 I talk you through some of the challenges of measuring results from coaching and ask you to think deeply about what you're really measuring and why that is important. In Chapter 11 I give you some tools to broaden your thinking further and catalyse your own ideas about what you are measuring and how you might measure it. These chapters introduce the part that systems play in results and the nature of variation.

In the final part the notion of systems is developed to understand how group coaching can be used to liberate talent and optimize the collective capabilities of everyone in the organization. In Chapter 12 I explore the talent system and how your strategy will direct your group coaching activities. Taking action for any coach is ultimately where the learning cements and takes hold, and in Chapter 13 I invite you to pick up the gauntlet and broaden the scope of the collective group to include the whole organization.

Your final destination

Accountability is what differentiates coaching from any other form of personal development – that you are going to be asked to review the actions you agreed to take and find out what worked and insights as to how, what didn't work and insights as to why, and if you didn't take any action, what it was that stopped you. The coaching process embedded within the book asks you to commit to doing something with what you've read and challenges you to take action. Talent optimization is an activity, and without applying the learning, talent will always remain dormant. So the final destination is really discovering what inspires you and ignites your energy so that you will take action.

PART ONE
The context of group coaching

Why it's important to start with self

Discovering the reasons you're interested in group coaching

Purpose, meaning, vocation and mission; these words conjure up different things for different people. I'm guessing that you don't wake up every morning wondering what the purpose of your work is. If we are to believe the statistics, the majority of employees go into work every day without really engaging in what they're doing. They are physically present but mentally they're somewhere else. In tough economic times there's a perceived view that people are 'waiting it out' till the economy improves before switching jobs. So why is that? You know the answer already – they are lacking purpose in what they do. Wouldn't it be great if through group coaching they could find a purpose for the work they do and feel engaged with the organization for which they work. And wouldn't it be great if organizations used group coaching as a means to activate their talent management strategy to create collegiate and collaborative working so that they could leverage all the talents of everyone in the organization. So do you know what your purpose is for group coaching? Think back to when you created your coaching philosophy. What was it in that philosophy that helped shape how you work with your clients? Was there something in there that was bigger than you or beyond what and who you are?

Having worked in a corporate environment for a large proportion of my working life I am well versed in the finer points of creating corporate mission statements. Just to be clear, that is not what we are talking about here. This is more visceral than fine words on a PowerPoint slide. This is about the higher value of coaching people in groups – what it does for you, how it shapes who you are and will become.

In Figure 1.1, I outline some of the things that point towards your purpose.

FIGURE 1.1

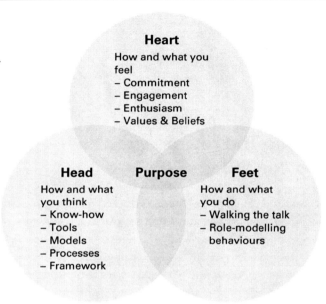

Heart
How and what you feel
– Commitment
– Engagement
– Enthusiasm
– Values & Beliefs

Head **Purpose** **Feet**

How and what you think
– Know-how
– Tools
– Models
– Processes
– Framework

How and what you do
– Walking the talk
– Role-modelling behaviours

Your purpose is greater than the sum of these parts and pulls together all the components to create your unique group coaching meaning. Bringing out your unconscious meaning to a purposeful awareness will help shape how you work with groups and how they experience you as their coach. Sure, you can be a good coach by just demonstrating skill and knowledge; if you want others to push themselves beyond what even they thought possible then you'll have to demonstrate that you've done that yourself. Coaching groups to liberate talent starts with taking yourself in hand and exploring your real purpose.

My group coaching purpose is to help people connect with others with their head, heart and inner strength – otherwise known as spirit – so that they have access to the capacity to grow and develop together. Anyone can be great given the right environment, support, process and opportunity to practise. I have a mission to work with organizations to help them tap into 100 per cent of their employees' potential so that they can grow ᴅᴏᴛ as individuals and as an organization, and this is how I define true talent management. Our purpose is defined by the legacy we create, and optimizing all the talents in a way that derives benefit from the collective and collaborative way in which those talents are put to use is what drives me. As individuals our legacy is the energy footprint we leave behind when we're no longer there – either because we've moved on to something or someplace new.

> Learning to live with another and to see oneself in the whole and see the whole in oneself. That learning to live with one another is all about being aware of our impact and our potential. That we're not alone, that we do exist in a world where there are other people... it's really about realizing potential and overcoming toleration, to see that living in our differences is actually a joyous and abundant experience.
>
> Lorna McDowell, MD Xenergie

What is the legacy that you want to leave behind?

Do you get where I'm coming from here? Your purpose drives you on even when times are tough, and gives you that added resilience to cope with things when they don't necessarily go according to plan. In those situations, my role as a group coach is to work with coachees and help them find ways to move from a position of feeling powerless, uncertain, helpless and stuck to a place where they are able to harness inner strength, create purposeful action and move forward towards their goal. My purpose helps me do just that. So you can see that having your own purpose clear and at the forefront of how you work with groups will define what type of group coach you are. Knowing your purpose and working out how you will manifest it is also about being clear on the means by which you will do so. Another coach, Angela Dunbar, who is a master of clean language coaching and emergent knowledge, delivers many of her group coaching sessions via the internet and teleclasses. Having experienced health and back problems, she wanted to find a way of working with people in groups that would reduce travel and yet allow her the opportunity to share her passion. And both of these aspects form part of her purpose:

I think there are two things – there's the fact that working in groups as opposed to one-to-one I personally find more energy-giving. I give energy but I get something back at the end of it. I can feel energized. If I had to travel halfway across the country to do it, then by the time I get back home I've lost some of that energy. But if I'm doing it this way [via the internet] I get to keep some of the energy – energy from the group. But there's also the energy I get from sharing my passion for clean coaching.

Knowing your purpose and being congruent is at the heart of authority and in the context of group coaching it is about the authority and credibility to work with coachees from a position of affinity: to demonstrate that you 'get them' at a deep level because you've done the work on yourself and are able to put yourself in their shoes. We will look at the coaching process later in the book; suffice to say that most coaching sessions start with an outcome. And as any coach will tell you, the outcome usually has importance attached to it and that's where purpose starts.

Finding your place on your journey

Clarity of purpose defines your group coaching journey and sets the scene for where you want to go and where you've come from. I've purposely used the word journey to get away from possibly more restrictive words like plan, strategy, steps or process because I want you to tap into the more creative and lateral part of your mind that knows stuff and will give you insights. Labelling it a plan or strategy at this stage might hinder unconscious processing; this is the start of the beginner's mindset.

Here's a simple exercise you can do for yourself and, if you like it, use with groups. And if you don't like it, get curious about what it is you don't like. Sometimes I purposely use tools that I don't like because not everyone is like me; and I've been amazed at how receptive others can be to stuff that I don't like.

The concept

Creating a spatial representation of your group coaching journey will trigger insights about what it means to you, where you've come from, where you want to go and how you might get there.

The exercise

1 Take a piece of paper and, allowing yourself just to go with the flow, put a mark on the paper of where you are now in relation to group coaching.

2 Now, put a mark on the paper of where you want to go in relation to group coaching.

3 Put a mark on the paper of where you've come from in relation to group coaching.

4 Next join the three marks together in whatever way that makes sense and looks ok to you.

5 What do you notice about:
   - The position on the page of the marks you've made – top, bottom, diagonally opposite, next to each other, close, far apart...?
   - The shape and size of the marks you made on the page – dots, squares, circles...?
   - The size of the paper you've chosen – is it a piece of flipchart paper, or is it a sticky note or maybe a piece of scrap paper that you had to hand...? Did you use one piece of paper?
   - The colour and type of pen you've chosen – is it a thick marker pen, a ballpoint pen, felt tip, blue, green, red...?
   - The type of connector you drew to join the three marks together – a straight line, zigzag line, wiggly line...?

6 Ask yourself these questions and any others that spring to mind:
   - What does this mean to you?
   - What insights do you have about how your mind represents your journey?
   - What does it say about your past, current and future journey in group coaching?
   - What can you take from the past and bring into the present?
   - How can you use what you know in the present to go forward into the future?
   - What did you feel about doing this exercise?
   - What beliefs were present as you read the text and then chose to do or not do the exercise?
   - How could you make this exercise even better?
   - How might you use it with groups?

Reflecting on what you've learnt from this simple exercise, start to make it come to life by adding in milestones, key facts along the way, anything that makes it real for you. For example, a key turning point for me in my journey was managing a team of people and experiencing the positive difference made by taking a coaching approach. I use this experience to shape my purpose and take it with me into the future to give meaning to the work I do with groups.

I have mentioned the beginner's mindset, and finding your place on your journey with group coaching is about continually appraising your own journey and reminding yourself both of how far you've come and the importance of keeping an open mind when working with groups. Curiosity is one of the greatest strengths a coach can have so the journey metaphor is also about exploration. Destination is important because knowing where you're going creates motivation and drive; that doesn't mean that you should ignore the landscape and occasionally go off-road exploring from time to time. After all, it has to be fun. And if you're enjoying what you're doing your enjoyment will rub off on others.

Understanding the scripts you might be running

This topic alone could fill another book and in fact in the references section I refer you to some great resources if you want to learn more. One of the prime directives of any coach is to create a safe space so it is with caution that I approach this subject, and I suggest that being aware of your own boundaries is crucial in using any tool that digs deep into the coachee's psyche. Having said that, it is important to understand your own 'stories' when working with groups, recognize any patterns of behaviour and explore what might be the cause with a view to doing something different. Coaching can be both remedial and generative. Yes, we need to explore the psyche to understand and gain awareness so that we can unlock potential, but the aim is not to analyse and heal: it is to use that awareness and take action. I will cover the contracting and qualification process later in the book, and just say here that as coaches we must be clear on our boundaries and be certain when coaching is the most appropriate intervention; in other words, if there's an underlying psychological issue then another approach might be considered, such as therapy or counselling.

So, having set the scene I want to explore the practical aspects of understanding the scripts you might be running and how they may or may not impact your group coaching approach. The background to the concept of life scripts was developed by Eric Berne in 1965 and forms part of his theory on transactional analysis. Essentially, the theory looks at how we 'transact' with others, that is to say how we interact with others, and what lies behind those interactions. In the context of group coaching this is probably one of the most accessible theories around social psychology, including personality, communication, systems and human development. It is also a helpful theory to understand the psychodynamics in the coaching relationship: what's happening in the relationship that we are unaware of at a conscious level and that we've brought with us from our childhood, and how this influences the way we now behave and interact with others. Imagine if you will, an electronic bridge between the unconscious and conscious mind – this bridge is constantly flowing with electric impulses that, although invisible, create energy in our day-to-day actions and words.

There are different perspectives on life scripts and Berne describes them as always negative in the sense that they are a self-fulfilling prophecy, a life plan that we fulfil, and are a key factor in depressive and addictive behaviours. In fact, he calls them the 'trash in our heads' (Berne, 1972). The word 'scripts' is now more commonly used, and more recent developments in the field of transactional analysis (Young, 1999) suggest that it is possible to re-write our scripts. And it is this aspect that I want to focus on and describe some of my strategies to create positive scripts that will support your activities when coaching groups. In my experience, working with groups is probably one of the most certain ways of discovering your own scripts and experiencing the phenomenon of 'what you think influences directly how you behave.'

So what does the word script conjure up for you? In transactional analysis terms the script is our life drama – in other words we create a play in which we have, usually, the principal role. As the playwright of our own lives we start to construct the drama in early childhood and attach meaning to the experiences we have that become vignettes in our play. So we have the plot, the script, the dialogue and the roles. Without over-analysing this and getting too deep, think back to a time when you were at your best and how your script might have helped you.

- What dialogue were you saying to yourself?
- Where did this dialogue come from?
- What experiences from your childhood might have helped you?
- Who were the people from your past that helped you be your best?

Having taken a detour along our journey, let's get practical and re-write the script. Your role as a group coach is exactly that, a role. It is not about who you are per se or your worth as a human being; it is about the work you are doing and the role you are playing. Liberating and optimizing talent starts with the premise that we all have the potential to develop. In other words, we all have equal value as human beings. The notion of your group coaching script as a play means that you will merely be performing a role in that play – it will not define you as a human being. Working with the concept of creating a positive script for your group coaching, let's look at the roles you'll be playing. The exercise at Figure 1.2 is a very simple way to help identify the different roles you'll be playing when group coaching. For example, one of your roles might be to nurture the group; another role might be to structure the group. There is no right or wrong answer; this exercise is as much about getting you to create the roles for your play as it is about understanding what's going on.

Read through what you've written and create a positive script for each of the roles that have a score of 8–10. For those that have a score of lower than 8 imagine that your score is 10 – what would the script be?

For example, when I'm at my best I have a mantra I repeat before starting the session: 'trust the process.' I also check myself when I feel my ego start to speak – this is either positive ('I am pleased this is going well') or negative ('I am feeling vulnerable because this isn't going well'). Both of these are conditional statements that make a judgement about me, not the role I am performing. When I hear these statements I reinforce the voice that says 'trust the process' and 'let go of the need for judgement.' Both of these last statements are my positive script for keeping my judgement at bay and re-minding me that I am performing a role. In doing this I am aspiring to keep the 'what' separate from the 'who'.

Boundary management is what it's all about and I find this helpful in evaluating my performance in the 'play'. How well we perform our roles is about skill, practice, technique, awareness and so on. To develop our group coaching talents, and help the people who we coach as well, requires of us a conscious approach to our own learning. Understanding our scripts and the roles we play makes this process more objective because it separates our positive self-regard from the roles we perform. When we mix up the two different aspects we recreate negative scripts that manifest in our beliefs and assumptions, and ultimately sap our confidence. Optimizing talent through group coaching requires the coach to model healthy self-regard and create an environment where it's ok not to give a star-studded performance all the

FIGURE 1.2

Role Question					
Who am I being when I'm in this role?					
Who am I not being when I'm in this role?					
Who/what would I like to be in this role?					
When I'm in this role, how similar/ dissimilar is it to my other roles?					
How happy am I in this role on a scale of 1–10 where 10 is Very Happy					
If not a 10, what stops it being a 10?					
What does this mean for me?					
What one thing will I do to increase my score?					
Other Questions relevant to you ....?					

time. That learning comes from assessing how well we've performed our role and re-learning our lines.

Assumptions, beliefs and confidence

Inherent in the scripts we run are the beliefs and assumptions that populate the stories within our plays. Without beliefs and assumptions we would find it difficult to operate; they provide a beacon that guides us and helps steer our life's course. That's not to say that all beliefs and assumptions are helpful. We each have beliefs and assumptions that block our true potential, either because they create a sense of fear or because they reinforce a presumption that 'Who are we to stand out and shine?' Think back to a time when you worked with a group and behind the words you heard a message of fear or lack of self-worth. These are the beliefs and assumptions that as a coach you have to master and find ways of harnessing, to transform that energy into a positive, driving force.

Self-doubt is surely one of the most pernicious assumptions because it saps confidence; often, when I've been at less than my best, it's because I've allowed negative beliefs and assumptions to creep in. And this is where you have to be really brutally honest with yourself about your own vulnerabilities. What are the beliefs and assumptions that you might hold that will stand in your way of being the best group coach you can be? These are the 'little voices' you hear in your head feeding you with messages.

Stream of consciousness exercise

- Sitting comfortably, allow your mind to feed you these voices. Listen to what they're saying and where they might be coming from.

- Write down each message as it comes to you. If you wish you can write each one on a separate Post-it note. Keep writing until you feel you've heard enough to make sense of the beliefs and assumptions that might stand in your way.

- If you've used Post-it notes you can then move the notes around and place them next to each other, above, below, in a different place in the room etc, to find out what effect that has on you internally; for example do you notice any physiological/mindset shifts when they're in different places? If so, what might this mean and how could you use this to help reshape the belief?

Let's draw out the positive messages from this exercise so that you have a useful resource to draw on when you need to dig deep into your reserves. Spend a few minutes answering these questions:

- What have you learnt about yourself from this exercise?

- What are you going to *do* with what you've learnt?

- How will you develop new habits, ie behaviours and actions?

- Positive assumptions and beliefs are important because...

- They will give me...

- So that I can...

When we work with coachees we will potentially make assumptions about their resourcefulness, willingness to learn, willingness to change behaviours, commitment, interest and so on. Be clear about your own beliefs and assumptions so that you have a battery of positive, energizing resources to draw upon. This will help maintain your confidence and allow you to hold the moments when you feel less brave so that you can find the true key to liberate your potential and act as a role model for others.

The egoless coach

This first chapter is about setting the scene for what follows – it's the groundwork for understanding how you can liberate talent in others through working collegiately and with a mindset of 'anything is possible given the support, means, opportunity and deliberate practice.' So what do I mean by the egoless coach? In order to be truly present in the coaching process you have to free yourself from your own need for recognition and self-importance. Many definitions of coaching refer to the coach as the 'invisible helper' – the coachees are unaware of your presence, absorbed instead by the coaching process and what it means for them. Sometimes this can be challenging for the coach because, being human, we have a need for recognition and this sometimes feels overpowering. Particularly when coaching individuals who externalize very little about their thoughts and feelings on the coaching process. And this is why I describe being a group coach as a journey – there will be many twists and turns and decision points along the way; having your own mental map of where you're going to help navigate those pinch points will make it more enjoyable and less tiring. There will be moments when your ego joins in the conversation and at that stage you need the perspicacity to acknowledge it and move one. The opposite end of the spectrum is the egocentric coach driven by their own needs and oblivious to the needs of the coachee. Egoless coaching taps into the 'higher self' that is able to put aside the coach's own needs in order to understand and truly hear the needs of the coachees.

In practical terms these are perhaps those moments when the coachees might challenge a question or react to something within the coaching process in an extreme way. In retaining an egoless state you are able to tap into your resourcefulness in order to explore with the coachees what has just happened rather than focusing on how the interaction has made you feel. And it also means that you have the option of bringing your own feelings into the coaching process in a productive way, for example sharing with the coachees what has just happened for you when they did or said something. This feedback may be useful data for the coachees or not, but the fact remains that it is now simply data that can be reviewed and assessed in the context of what has just happened. In keeping your ego out of the way you are able to retain a state of resourcefulness that ultimately is going to be most helpful both for the coachees and for you.

I've listed below some of my descriptions of egoless qualities; add your own based on what egoless means to you:

- humility;
- willingness to take risks;
- empathy;
- magnanimity;
- authenticity;
- congruence;
- self-awareness;
- and...

Essentially, being an egoless coach means that you are grounded in who you are. Another way of saying this is that you are comfortable in your own skin and it is ok for coachees to be themselves and explore their awareness of self in a safe environment. It's likely you'll be coaching from an egoless state if you as the group coach have a clear purpose, are willing to experiment with ideas and tools even when they feel uncomfortable or unfamiliar to you, know what is going on in your head and can work positively with your own beliefs and assumptions without stressing too much, and most of all eschew praise and glory.

Stretching people beyond their comfort zone to engage them and develop talents means they have to feel there is a purpose to it. Talent management in the broadest sense is about igniting excitement and engagement for the discovery and exploration process even though the coachees might be a bit apprehensive. Coachees have to feel there is a benefit in taking that step and really digging deep to liberate their talents. And so the next chapter explores the benefits that are possible from group coaching for everyone, including the coach.

KEY POINTS

- Be clear on your own purpose for group coaching so that you are able to coach others to find theirs.

- Be vigilant about managing your physical and emotional state and conscious of where your boundaries lie within the coaching agenda.

- Understand the scripts you might be running so that you can develop awareness of what scripts your coachees might be playing out.

- Be brutally honest with yourself about where you feel vulnerable and create beliefs and assumptions that will support your growth and development as a coach.

- The prime directive of the coach is to create a safe space for coachees to work.

- Keep your ego out of the way in order to stay resourceful.

02 Benefits of group coaching

Defined benefits

Is there enough in this to make it worth your while? Ultimately that's what a benefit is about. Balancing what you're going to have to put in against what you're going to get out. If you are thinking of adopting group coaching as part of your talent management strategy, this is an area that you should explore in depth, taking into account the wider organizational system. In Part Four I explore some of the questions around how you measure the results of coaching and this chapter is really the start of that process. But a benefit is very different from a result. Coaches can sometimes enter what I call a 'somnambulistic coaching state' – it's the one where the coach colludes with both the client and the coachees about 'We all know what we're going to get out of this' as they trot out the usual: increased performance, changed behaviours and so on. In fact, these are the results – they're not necessarily the benefits that any of the parties is going to gain. Benefits are more subtle and not always likely to rise naturally to the surface, and can even sometimes be out of the person's awareness. This is one of the reasons for having a more robust and in-depth conversation about the overt and hidden benefits that each party wants from the coaching, including the coach's own gain.

Looking at the definition of the word 'benefit' there are four possible characteristics that might make something worthwhile:

- that it's favourable to you (and/or possibly others);
- that you will obtain some sort of advantage;
- that it will be helpful in some way;
- that you will profit from it – these could be tangible or intangible gains.

These will probably be different for each party included in the coaching dynamic. For example, there may well be a difference between the benefits that the group as a whole might gain and the benefits for each individual. Recognizing these dynamics and tensions at the start of the engagement is crucial to both the way that the coaching develops and how each party will measure its value. And I use the word value because something can and does have value even if it isn't a success (in whatever way the person defines success). In this chapter we'll look at the answers to these questions for all parties involved.

The virtuous or vicious triangle

Great stories always have a dynamic tension between the 'goody' and the 'baddy' and, without making too many judgements, this is probably a good place to start a discussion about how people behave with others, and perhaps more importantly, how people behave in systems. The psychodynamics of any relationship are based on our 'life positions' in the sense that we have a pattern of behaviour. This pattern typically reveals itself when faced with challenging situations or situations that we perceive as challenging. The flight, fight, freeze response gets played out in different ways in group coaching, and the identification of benefits hints at these patterns. Sometimes payoffs are disguised as benefits. In transactional analysis Steve Karpman developed a diagrammatic way of illustrating the destructive transaction with others that can occur: the drama triangle. The three roles in this drama are: persecutor, victim and rescuer. Figure 2.1 is a pictorial representation of these roles. We will explore the playing out of this drama in the group scenario later in the book. The purpose here is to examine how payoffs can sometimes be misconstrued as benefits.

FIGURE 2.1

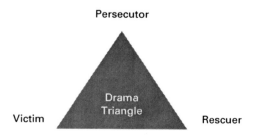

So some potential payoffs for a victim might be:

- They receive attention.
- They can abdicate responsibility for solving their own problems.
- They bolster support against their persecutor.

These payoffs mean that they never resolve the underlying issue: the cause of their victim status. And when their rescuer doesn't do what they expect, they can take on the role of persecutor against their rescuer. The distinction between payoff and benefit is important because there might not be a benefit to the individual of learning new behaviours if they're already getting payoffs from their current pattern. When you think about the potential benefits for the different parties engaged in the group coaching it might be worth creating two columns – one headed payoffs and the other headed benefits.

Sometimes organizational clients have clearly defined expectations of the benefits likely to accrue from group coaching – these may well undercut the payoffs that individuals are receiving from their current behaviour patterns. For example, one individual I worked with flipped between victim and persecutor mode in order to safeguard their perceived status in the organization. The intervention of group coaching brought this to the surface and the real benefit of the intervention – collaborative working – was not achieved. The individual would have to entertain a level of vulnerability that for this person did not have sufficient benefit to outweigh the payoff of their current behaviour pattern.

Benefits from group coaching accrue when the drama is transformed into a journey (Figure 2.2).

FIGURE 2.2

The challenger, explorer and listener are roles along the journey that open up the possibility of a discussion around allowing vulnerability, recognizing that individuals will be challenged and that they are expected to listen at a deep level. So in the example above, a conversation at the beginning of the engagement might sound like this:

> One of the benefits I might gain is a deeper understanding of what causes my behaviour through exploring my vulnerability and allowing myself to be challenged.

It is important to 'out' subtle differences between payoffs and benefits at an early stage; otherwise the group coach might encounter the vicious drama triangle in their sessions. The virtuous journey triangle is a counter to this potential drama, and later in the book I will share some more tools and techniques and some from other group coaches. It takes courage to get to this level of subtlety and it's sometimes too easy to sleepwalk your way through the engagement process. The dynamics of how we interact with others are complex and fascinating; one of the benefits for me of coaching groups is the opportunity to observe and learn more about what makes us tick.

The power dynamic around status and authority also impacts the expected benefits and the balance of gains made. We have already established that authority, whether it is perceived or actual, is a key influencer on our behaviour. Figure 2.3 illustrates a relationship of equals in the coaching scenario. The group coaching dynamic is more sophisticated than one-to-one coaching; hence it's represented by two equilateral triangles joined together. Here's a simple way of thinking about this – imagine a rubber band between each of the parties: the amount of tension between each party is the same.

FIGURE 2.3

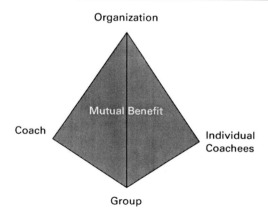

Consider Figure 2.4 and have a think about what might have caused the change. What might be happening to the tension in the rubber band?

FIGURE 2.4

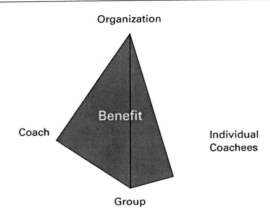

For those with a more numerical preference, imagine that the benefits to each party have changed as follows:

- Organization – 30 per cent.
- Coach – 30 per cent.
- Group – 30 per cent.
- Individual coachees – 10 per cent.

By the way, you might want to consider testing this out with a real rubber band. And it might be a great tool to use with coachees and clients so that they have an experience of what the tension might feel like as well. Sometimes very simple physical activities like this work really well. I am constantly surprised by how much value and discussion can be generated by the simplest exercise.

The dynamic tension in the benefits each party accrues may stem from dramas that are being enacted or power dynamics at play. The role of the group coach is to explore these with all parties so that well-defined benefits are identified up front. This may well lead to some uncomfortable conversations – for the coach as well – that might result in the need for a different type of intervention or a 'no go' decision from any of the parties. Ultimately it's about understanding what someone will gain from doing something different, rather than the payoff they're getting from staying where they are.

Benefits elicitation exercise

Let's start exploring the possible specific benefits from group coaching. I've turned the definitions outlined earlier in the chapter into questions as a starting point to discuss with your potential coachees and clients and to use for yourself. One of the suggestions is to listen deeply and explore whether these are real benefits or payoffs.

- How might participating in group coaching be favourable to you (and/or possibly others)?
- Why is that important to you?
- What advantage do/might you wish to obtain?
- Why is that important to you?
- How will it be helpful?
- Why is that important to you?
- In what way is it helpful?
- How will you profit from it? (These could be tangible or intangible gains.)
- What payoffs might you gain from *not* participating in coaching?
- Why are these important to you?
- How might you define payoffs? Give me some real life examples.
- How might you define benefits? Give me some real life examples.
- Which feels better, a payoff or a benefit?

You could also use scaling questions as well to identify relative importance, eg 1–10 where 10 is very important/desirable.

The benefits and gains for each party

Benefits and gains are highly personalized – even in the context of the organization. After all, the clients represent the organization; they are not the organization itself. So this last section explores what the potential benefits might be and is designed as an aid for discussion rather than a definitive list. The most satisfying experiences of working with groups come from having a deep understanding of what each individual wants to gain. That deep understanding starts with the group coach developing an intense curiosity that characterizes the beginner's mindset. Practising this mindset through the exploration of those gains is a great place to start.

Benefits for coachees

Step into the shoes of the coachee for a few minutes and imagine that you have been asked to participate in a group coaching programme. Allow your mind to explore every nook and cranny and start to write (or draw) freely, without judgement. What are the benefits you want as the coachee? Do this exercise first before looking at what I've come up with.

What do you notice about your answers? What did you hear yourself saying as you read through your answers? Did you notice any changes in your physiology? Were you surprised by anything? How might you use these answers to inform your group coaching practice? What might these answers suggest to you about your assumptions?

Here are my answers. I did this exercise using Post-it notes and a flipchart to look at what was in front of me. I then prioritized the Post-it notes and here are the exact words I'd written on the Post-its:

1 Have time out of the day just to think.
2 Social interaction.
3 Gain tools and techniques and experience how to put my point of view across powerfully.
4 It would be helpful to know what I'm doing in the group and how I come across.
5 Raise my visibility.
6 Maybe find out about possible opportunities elsewhere in the organization/market.

It might be interesting to spend a few minutes reflecting on the similarities and differences between both sets of answers. What might have influenced our answers? It's likely that our own experiences of the world will have shaped our responses. When I did this exercise I had no idea what might come up, so it's quite interesting to reflect that time to think is number one. I have a suspicion that this reflects the reality of most of my clients – that there's never enough time in the day to just sit down and reflect.

Benefits for the clients

Who is the client? Sometimes the client and the coachee is one and the same – particularly if you offer an online group coaching programme. The probability is that the person who's enrolled in the programme will also be paying for the service. So it might be that they have dual benefits: one set for them personally as the coachee, and the advantages that their business will gain as a result. In an organizational setting the client could be the manager of the coachee, it could be the HR person, it could be a programme manager who's been assigned to manage a specific programme of which group coaching forms part. In any of these scenarios the benefits are likely to have a different perspective from the coachee's; but there might also be some overlap.

Do the same exercise again but this time write down (or draw) the benefits for each person's role as well as the organization or business. You can approach this in a number of ways; for example, take one role at a time or brainstorm all possible benefits onto Post-its and allocate to roles afterwards.

Here are my answers:

- Coachee's manager:
  - develop them for their next role;
  - enable others to share experiences 'in team';
  - enable people to solve their own problems... which means less workload (for me!) (is this a payoff?);
  - makes me look good because I'm developing my people;
  - makes it easier to manage the person;
  - helps them get another perspective;
  - more productive/happier team.
- HR Manager:
  - reduce conflict and improve working relationships;
  - better collaborative working;
  - more visibility for me;
  - help people understand how to manage other people... which means (a) less workload (for me!) (is this a payoff?); and (b) development of talent.
- Programme manager:
  - more innovation/ideas;
  - transfer learning to others;
  - greater commitment to goals;
  - a 'programme' identity;
  - kudos – for me as the programme manager and for the coachees;
  - more innovation/ideas;
  - transfer learning to others;

- Organization:
  - more innovation/ideas;
  - greater commitment to goals;
  - reduce conflict and improve working relationships;
  - better collaborative working;
  - transferable learning experiences;
  - knowledge and experience sharing;
  - increase engagement in the organization... which means that
    (a) productivity will be as a result of 'flow' state; and
    (b) the organization will be better able to cope with change.

What have you put for your answers? You might notice that some of the benefits overlap and that some of them have a direct gain for the person in the role, or you might not. These answers will also be shaped by your experiences and the filters you operate with. The key thing is recognizing that benefits are context and content specific and the individuals shape their own world based on the experiences they've had.

What does this mean for you as the group coach? It might be that you approach each assignment with fresh eyes and thoughts. Yes, the client may well tell you things that seem very similar to other clients you've worked with before, but dig deeper and you may find very individual benefits that they're hoping to accrue from engaging in group coaching.

Benefits for you, the coach

Finally we come to the benefits that you, the coach, will gain from coaching groups. For me there are probably three things:

- learning something new each time I engage with a group;
- challenging my own comfort zone so that I keep that 'beginner's mindset';
- connecting with others who have different perspectives to practise open-minded thinking.

There is something about working with a group that means the energy starts to come back at you somehow, because it's amplified by the presence of other people. So if you're doing group coaching, although you might be facilitating it's not all coming from you. So I think from my perspective it uses up less energy.

Angela Dunbar, master clean language and emergent knowledge coach

What are the top three benefits you will gain from group coaching? I am guessing they will be different from mine. Ultimately, they will be personal and shaped by the experiences you've had and what's important to you. Mine are driven by a need to keep the 'ego' out of the group coaching; ironically, when I keep 'me' out of it I'm at my best. Ultimately, the benefit of group coaching for me is that it teaches humility and, without seeming paradoxical, humility is something I constantly aspire to in all my coaching and consultancy practices.

Being clear about the benefits you expect from group coaching means you have taken a systematic approach to enabling talent development. It's the second step in purpose definition: the first step is understanding why it's important to use group coaching and the second step answers 'so that...' The greater degree of certainty and congruence between the 'why' and the 'so that', the higher the chance of realizing your vision. The same applies to understanding the specific activities you'll undertake to reap the rewards. The next chapter explores the way group coaching is defined to help you establish even more certainty.

KEY POINTS

- Effort required versus benefit accrued determines the level of engagement; the greater the benefits, the higher the level of engagement.

- Benefits may not always be obvious either to you, the coachee or the client so it's important to explore these thoroughly at the engagement stage.

- Group coaching increases the complexity of the coaching dynamic and creates a tension between balancing the differing parties' expectations around benefits.

- Benefits and gains are personal, and even if a client or coachee acknowledges an objective benefit there may well be a subjective benefit for them personally, eg potential promotion opportunities.

03

Certainty drives action

Getting clear on definitions

What is coaching? Isn't it just another word for training, mentoring, consulting, counselling? If you ask anyone what coaching is you're likely to get this type of response. Defining coaching is the first activity for anyone new to the field of coaching. In fact, it is likely you already have a definition of coaching up your sleeve if you're a trained coach. And you'll no doubt have a set of ready-prepared answers to the question: How does coaching differ from mentoring, training, counselling, consultancy etc? If not, then I offer these simple exercises to help lubricate the synapses. I have used these many times for all sorts of subjects and they seem to work particularly well for definitions.

Exercise

Taking a piece of flipchart paper, divide it into three chunks horizontally. Figure 3.1 illustrates what it might look like.

1 On the top chunk write the word 'Mentoring', on the middle chunk 'Coaching' and on the lowest chunk 'Counselling'.

2 Quickly write or draw what comes to mind for each activity – what characterizes it and distinguishes it as an activity?

3 Looking at what you've come up with, what strikes you about the boundaries for each activity?

4 If you were to draw a timeline, where might you draw the past, present and future?

5 Where does each activity sit on that timeline?

FIGURE 3.1

Mentoring
Coaching
Counselling

I've completed my own version of this with my ideas of what characterizes each (Figure 3.2). I've distilled what I think is the purpose to each as well. These are my thoughts and are not the only way to look at these activities, so have a look at what you've come up with and get curious about where your ideas are different from or similar to mine.

An alternative exercise is to see where the overlaps are:

1   Draw three circles that overlap each other as in Figure 3.3.

2   On each circle write an activity: Mentoring, Coaching, Counselling.

3   Write or draw the unique activities in the activity circle and the overlapping activities in the joins.

4   What sits across all three circles?

FIGURE 3.2

Future

Present

Past

Mentoring – To share experience and wisdom to support development of mentee in their career or specialism
Sharing experiences
Guiding mentee through a process
Suggesting resources to explore
Connecting to their networks
Providing a sounding board
Helping mentee explore and navigate organizational politics
Providing 'in the moment' feedback
Helping set career goals
Working back from the future to create the best career path
Focus on planning for the future

Purpose: Career/specialism development

Coaching – To facilitate learning and self-awareness of the coachee to unlock potential
Sharing tools and models
Asking questions and listening
Providing 'in the moment' feedback
Reflecting back to the coachee
Helping set goals and outcomes for the coaching
Encouraging action and holding to account
Fostering coachee-led learning
Working on the present to create the future
Focus on taking action
Holding the space for the coachee to explore and experience

Purpose: Personal development

Counselling – To enable awareness and closure to help the client move on
Sharing insights about the past and how it impacts the present
Using therapeutic models to assist equilibrium
Asking questions and listening
Reflecting back
Exploring cause of current anxiety/situation
Holding the space for the client to explore and experience
Focus on letting go of the past to reach closure and moving on

Purpose: Improve mental health and well-being

FIGURE 3.3

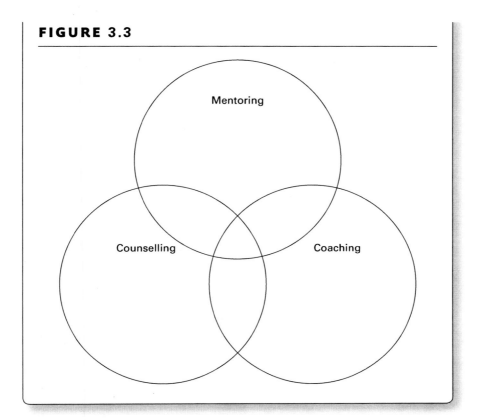

These two quick exercises illustrate that there are shared skills across all of these activities and there are characteristics that are unique and define the activity. For example, it is very unlikely that advice will feature in either exercise for coaching, whereas it is likely to feature in mentoring. If you were to include consultancy in the exercise then advice would also feature there as well. Sometimes it's helpful to start with the question: 'What is coaching *not* about?'

Consider using these exercises as an introduction to your coaching group since you will probably already have clarity about these terms. It's a useful way to help establish what is in and out of scope for the group coaching. I have found that these exercises generate a lot of discussion and get people to think about their own experiences of when they've had mentoring or coaching and, if they're willing to disclose, counselling. Real-life experience adds colour to the definitions and allows you to get specific.

If the term 'coaching' seems to be hard to pin down then the terms 'talent' and 'talent management' will provide endless hours of amusement. 'Talent management' as an activity has been around for about 20 years. Here's my radical definition of 'talent management':

> Talent management, therefore, is the whole range of tools, techniques, approaches, strategies, policies, processes and technology a business can use to increase engagement and influence the psychological contract it has with its employees. Done well, this leads to high-performing, productive and enthusiastic employees who feel proud to work for their organization, and find purpose and meaning for where they spend a good proportion of their life (2011).

Here's my definition of talent:

> Talent is latent potential and when we describe someone as talented this means they've actualized that potential.

David Shenk (2011) provides an elegant solution to understanding the word, talent: 'It is a linguistic apparition.' And the same can be said about the word 'coaching'.

So why is it so important to define these terms? There's an inherent paradox operating here: on the one hand you need to be clear on the definitions to help develop an overarching framework on which to hang your coaching; on the other hand you need to know how to navigate the gaps between (as in the second exercise). The definitions both provide certainty and pinpoint overlap and blurring of boundaries. Group coaches who demonstrate both flexibility and comfort when working with uncertainty and a strong sense of personal boundaries elicit willingness in the groups they coach to stretch beyond their comfort zones. That's not to say that you should take foolhardy risks with either the people you are coaching or your own professionalism. It's about encouraging a growth mindset by gently helping coachees out of their comfort zones and enabling them to acknowledge that sometimes it's ok not to know. After all, that elicits the question: 'Shall we find out?' All of this is predicated on having a strong contracting process and clarity on the ground rules, otherwise known as 'how we'll work together'.

Let's turn to the term 'group coaching'. This is a relatively new term, although the practice has been around for a while. In *50 Top Tools For Coaching* (2009) I comment that coaching is something that can be traced back to ancient times in the form of Socrates, the classical philosopher. The way that Socrates explores the meaning of commonly held ideals is a model of both coaching and group coaching in its simplest form. The group coach, Socrates, through the use of questioning, listening and feedback provides an environment in which a group of individuals can learn together (the group Socrates coached comprised Athenian citizens who were exclusively young and male). The act of observing another's learning process means we can learn ourselves. So a simple definition of coaching could be:

> Coaching is the application of questioning, listening and feedback to enable the learning and self-development of another whilst putting your own specific needs and learning to one side.

Here's a simple definition of group coaching:

> Group coaching is the application of questioning, listening and feedback facilitated by the coach to enable the mutual learning and self-development of a group of individuals whilst putting your own specific needs and learning as the coach to one side.

The fact that the coach is likely to learn as well is the parallel process that happens in coaching. We inadvertently learn something about ourselves even when our aim is to help another. Group coaching is an environment in which the sum of the parts is greater than the whole and is a manifestation of parallel processing. Individual coaching enables the client to have 'Aha!' moments that shine light onto areas of their life hitherto either unknown or in confusion. Group coaching has the potential to create exponential 'Aha!' moments because one person's experience can cause a chain reaction in others that is linked only tangentially to the original individual's experience. The role of the group coach is to draw out this shared learning experience to leverage the sum of the parts.

Exercise

If you haven't done so already, write down your definition of coaching. Read it out loud. What do you want/need to add or change to make it your working definition of group coaching?

At this stage it is your definition that counts. In the following section we'll explore what others say about coaching and group coaching so that you can compare your definition with others. It is a fact that there are many definitions of coaching, each with a different nuance – none is right or wrong, they're just definitions that make sense to their authors. The key reason for having a definition is that it provides you and your clients with clarity on what you and they can expect, understanding of the coaching boundaries and encourages joint responsibility for creating the relationship.

How coaching has been defined

Now that you have your own definition of coaching and group coaching, let's look at other definitions. The first definition, by Anthony Grant of the University of Sydney, is the one used by the Association for Coaching. The third definition, by Myles Downey, is the one often used by coaches and authors.

> A collaborative solution-focused, results-orientated and systematic process in which the coach facilitates the enhancement of work performance, life experience, self-directed learning and personal growth of the coachee (Association for Coaching).

> Coaching is partnering with clients in a thought-provoking and creative process that inspires them to maximize their personal and professional potential (International Coaching Federation).

> Coaching is the art of facilitating the development, learning and performance of another (Downey, 2003).

Having read through these definitions how do they compare with your own? As you will see there are common threads to these definitions. What might be the implications for the coaching practice of these authors? How might their definitions shape their coaching? And what implications do your own definitions have for your coaching practice? How do these definitions link back to your coaching philosophy and purpose?

Let's turn to the definition of group coaching to explore how this compares.

> As for personal coaching, but the coach is working with a number of individuals either to achieve a common goal within the group, or create an environment where individuals can co-coach each other (Association for Coaching).

> A small-group process throughout which there is the application of coaching principles for the purposes of personal or professional development, the achievement of goals, or greater self-awareness, along thematic or non-thematic lines (Britton, 2010).

> A facilitated process led by a skilled professional coach and created with the intention of maximizing the combined energy, experience and wisdom of individuals who choose to join in order to achieve organizational objectives and/or goals (Cockerham, 2011).

There is a mutuality of benefit from group coaching – the combination of joint intellectual and emotional energy of the group that helps deliver greater outcomes and results. The hypothesis of this book is that this experience and outcome can be leveraged to develop talent. Another benefit therefore of group coaching is that it presents a greater opportunity for systemic learning and the chance that, in learning how to work with others, group members can tap into their hidden potential. This shared experience has the capability to catalyse and create a viral learning experience across the organization.

Team and group coaching

The other conundrum with any definition of group coaching is: where does team coaching fit? Labels can create confusion but that's not to deny that there are differences between team and group coaching. In reality there is little difference in the dynamics of group and team coaching – you are working with a collection of individuals and because of that there will be interpersonal dynamics at play. Possibly the main difference is that team coaching is likely to be with a collection of individuals who already work together and are likely to continue to do so (usually towards a shared objective) whereas coaching a group means they're likely to be individuals who don't usually work together. It's worth noting that groups do share an objective around learning together, so in that sense they become a team for the duration of the group coaching. Team coaching may be working with a pre-existing or newly formed team to help them be more effective as a team, whereas group coaching is more likely to be with a disparate collection of individuals or an action-learning group that is working to reinforce and embed new behaviours.

Figure 3.4 gives a summary of some of the differences.

Facilitation and group coaching

Here's the next quandary: where does facilitation sit in this equation? Is facilitation the same as group coaching or is it different? Again, we return to our old friend 'purpose'. The purpose of facilitation is:

> To help bring about change or movement whilst enabling the people within the group to learn for themselves how to work more productively.

This self-directed change or movement elicits content and learning from the group. Looking back at the definition and purpose of group coaching, this

FIGURE 3.4

Team coaching	Group coaching
For: – Established teams working together long term – New or newly merged teams	**For:** – Groups of individuals drawn together temporarily as a team – Sometimes larger groups geographically spread – Cross-functional teams responsible for delivering joint goals
Who want to: – Identify and achieve unified goals – Achieve mutually beneficial results – Improve teamworking, collaboration and performance	**Who want to:** – Achieve mutually beneficial results – Improve teamworking, collaboration and performance – Embed learning following development programme – Share knowledge and provide mutual support – Develop best-practice groups by joint learning from one another – Build systemic awareness
Possible outcomes: – Identifying business direction, goals, obstacles, solutions and actions – Improved accountability, respect, trust and understanding – Increased accountability and 'buy in' – Improved teamwork and collaboration – Honest, authentic dialogue – Shared knowledge and learning	**Possible outcomes:** – Shared knowledge and learning and reinforcement – Deepened knowledge through sharing practice – Peer support and co-coaching network – Increased accountability – Cross-functional understanding, teamwork and increased collaboration

SOURCE: Cockerham, Hawkins *et al*

is very similar. It might be controversial but I assert that group coaching is the same as facilitation provided the facilitator or coach leaves their ego at the door. I have experienced some facilitation that seeks to elevate the status of the facilitator through the use of 'war stories' and too many pet theory models. This level of content and direction lends itself more to a group mentoring role.

What about training? Sometimes this borders on group coaching – particularly where the learners seek self-knowledge rather than pure subject knowledge or skills training. The boundaries can sometimes become blurred, and in this scenario it is apparent that the method of training delivery probably rests more in the facilitation/group coaching camp than 'chalk and talk'. Training typically tends to be high in content and instruction. There are specific theories, models or ideas to be delivered to the group so that they can learn and apply them.

Boundary management

Advancements in neuroscience suggest the prime directive of the mind is certainty. That is one of the reasons human beings experience discomfort during times of change – the quantity required will vary among individuals, but the overall need for certainty is universal. So what is the benefit of allowing a blurring of the boundaries for the activities of group coaching? When might it be ok to get more into content? When might it not be ok? How do you as the coach know when it's ok? What is happening that provides data on which to base your judgement? How long do you allow the group to struggle with a topic or issue before providing input or another intervention? The ability to judge what intervention and when to apply it is a core competence of coaching, facilitation, consultancy, training and counselling; this is something that happens in the moment and sometimes goes well and sometimes doesn't. Each time provides an opportunity for everyone to learn if it's brought into the awareness of all concerned. To help navigate this tricky path, here's a quick model that you can use to assess where you typically prefer to operate. You can also use it as a reflection tool after each coaching session or specific intervention. It's based on a four-box model and the two continuums are process versus content and directive versus non-directive. I have marked my preferences on the model so you can see how it works (Figure 3.5).

FIGURE 3.5

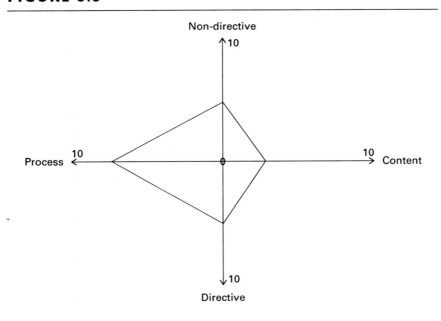

Exercise

1 On a scale of 1–10, how much attention do you pay to the process in your coaching?

2 On a scale of 1–10, how much content do you give to your coachees?

3 On a scale of 1–10, how much direction do you give to your coachees? (This could be in terms of the exercises you use and range through to telling them how to do something.)

4 On a scale of 1–10, how much do you stand back and let the coachees work under their own initiative, ie exploring what and how for themselves?

Note down your scores on the relevant continuum and then join up the dots! You will see that my model of group coaching is skewed towards process and has a balance of directive and non-directive behaviours. I will sometimes give content, and this is usually where the coachees have either asked for help and it's clear that they're at the 'unconscious incompetence' learning stage or where I've noticed something in the group and made a suggestion. I always caveat any suggestion with: 'This is just a thought and you are free to choose whether to go with it or use it to catalyse other ideas – I am very comfortable if you want to go with something else.' It is intriguing how this can sometimes provide a break in their behaviours that then seems to spark a new burst of energy to explore something entirely different.

Boundary management is important and awareness of when the boundaries are becoming blurred is integral to applying sound judgement. As the coach, you never know exactly what is likely to help; provided you keep yourself free from emotional engagement in the content this will ensure you maintain objectivity and stay resourceful.

Coaching isn't therapy – although it can be therapeutic

Blurry boundaries present an opportunity to explore some of the more therapeutic practices within group coaching and the growing interest in therapeutic models applied to business settings. One in particular, mindfulness, is gaining great popularity. Mindfulness has evolved from ancient Buddhist meditative practices adapted to a secular form. The practice of mindfulness helps develop and create awareness of the present, from both an intrapersonal and an environmental perspective. The therapeutic application is primarily concerned with people suffering with depression and stress, and what research has shown is that it also benefits overall well-being.

In a busy schedule it is easy to fall into the habit of thinking ahead to the next thing 'to do' on the agenda for the day, without truly appreciating the present. In a group coaching setting, it is likely that coachees will arrive at the session with at least 101 things on their mind. Applying some of the practices of mindfulness enables the coachees to be present both physically and mentally. Later on we will look at some of the techniques for enabling this. The coach is the 'pause' button on their day that allows them to unwind and take stock so that the coachees have increased resourcefulness. The coach is not a therapist but is using proven techniques to help engender a sense of well-being. After all, we know intuitively that we perform and interact much better when we are feeling good about ourselves and have a heightened level of self-worth.

Mindfulness is a great way of helping coachees find purpose and clarity because it creates a space in which they can explore what's going on for them in the 'here and now'. So definitions of what is and isn't coaching will help create a scope for the work to be done, but the definition shouldn't be so solid that it denies the benefits from other fields of expertise. Navigating the difference between a therapeutic model of working with groups versus a coaching perspective enriches the experience for everyone.

Knowing what you want and where you're going

If certainty drives action then the two group coaching continua have implications for your role as the group coach. You as the coach have to take responsibility to choose your role and then be accountable for what happens. Do you want to operate more at the 'content' and 'directive' sides of the model? Or do you choose to work from the 'process' and 'non-directive' quadrants? If the former, then it's likely you will operate from an 'expert' perspective, and the latter from a 'facilitator' perspective. Or are you happy moving between the two, depending on the context? The key elements are choice and flexibility.

Let's return to the 'egoless' coach concept. All of the choices we make in the group coaching activities and relationship must come from a client-centred or client-driven approach, not from our own egocentric needs, if we are to serve our coachees well. Look back at your definitions of coaching and group coaching. How much of 'you' is in that definition? What's important to you when you work with coachees? Do you need to be seen as the content expert or the expert on the coaching process? And be honest with yourself here. Awareness of our own needs is paramount because we then have choice to do something about it. Coaching ultimately is about responsibility – or response-ability as I prefer to call it. It's about enabling the coachee to reach solution or resolution on their own and make choices about what they do or don't do with that insight and knowledge.

KEY POINTS

- There are many definitions of coaching and group coaching. Each definition describes characteristics that are important to a specific coach. Develop your own definition that links to your purpose so that you have a guide to provide certainty for you and your clients.

- Definitions help provide boundaries. These boundaries create expectations and help you and your coachees work through coaching in a way that has meaning for you and for them.

- Understand where the differences and similarities lie with other fields of expertise in mentoring, counselling, training and consultancy.

- Acknowledge that these areas of expertise may have approaches that could be adapted to group coaching, and manage the paradox of staying true to your boundaries whilst retaining flexibility.

PART TWO
Creating a group coaching strategy

Group coaching process

04

Before you go into a state of apoplexy about the word 'strategy' take a deep breath! Strategy is an overused word that can turn otherwise self-confident and smart people into panicking, dithering wrecks. Here's my simple definition:

> A strategy is an overarching, decisive course of action that will lead you to your objective.

So it's a plan with a purpose. Deciding on a strategy means that you're committing time, resources and energy to that course of action in preference to any other course of action. By now, you'll have realized the importance of purpose and definitions – they will tell you which course of action to take and help you make decisions about what you will and won't do as a group coach. So your strategy is all about turning that purpose and definition into action. How you do that is through your group coaching process; your strategy is the start point for creating that process. It is an input to the steps you will take and the outputs you hope might ensue. Notice I say hope, because one of the reasons for creating a process is that it enables you to measure data that tell you how well your process delivers your strategy.

So what is a process? All coaches use a process – they maybe don't realize it but essentially any coaching model or tool usually takes the form of a process. Here's my definition of a process:

> A collection of related tasks that through a series of steps act on input to create output.

Figure 4.1 is an illustration of what a simple process might look like. The aim of this chapter is to help you create your own group coaching process. Process mapping is an art form in itself and there are many resources online if you wish to find out more about developing your skills

FIGURE 4.1

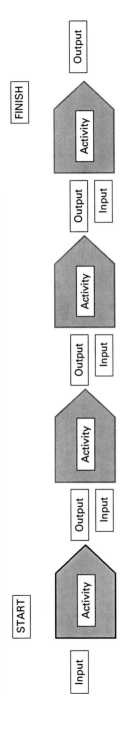

in this area. I've listed some of them in the resources section. My aim is to create a simple process that enables you to replicate success and learn – from both the good and the not so good. There are essentially two measures of a process: efficiency and effectiveness. How quickly you work through your process is a measure of how efficient the process is. In group coaching terms this may or may not be important. Think about this though: if you knew that you could achieve the same results quicker but in a different way, would you change your process? Is time an important resource for your clients? There is a downside to measuring just the speed of your process because you might miss out the qualitative aspects of your group coaching – how well the outcomes are achieved. So you might be able to run speedy group coaching sessions but people might leave the session feeling that their outcomes have not been met. So you need both measures to understand how your process performs. This data helps you improve the process and is the core reason for working with a process as opposed to a tick list.

A tick list is great for reminding yourself what to cover in the session and as an aid to brainstorming all the topics and activities you wish to cover.

Exercise

Spend a few minutes creating a list of things that you could do in a group coaching session. The aim here is to write quickly and just jot things down as they come to mind. When you've developed your list, have a look at it. If you went into a group coaching session with that list, how would you know where to start? Which of those things on your list are important or a priority? And at the end of the session how would you know what you did so that you could replicate it at another session?

A tick list is a great input tool for your process but it doesn't help you:

- work out the flow of activities;

- determine a critical path;

- identify outputs;

- keep you focused on the start and end point;

- help you replicate what you've done;

- identify areas that need to be changed/improved;

- allow opportunities to add/remove things based on what you've learnt.

A process helps create a path and scope for the coaching. In effect, it is another way of creating a natural boundary around the group coaching activity. It helps you as the group coach focus on the coachees because you can free yourself from worrying about where things might go. I mentioned the inner voice earlier in the book and one of the mantras I recite to myself is 'Trust the process'. The more groups you coach, the more you will experience that the process delivers certain behaviours. For example, many years ago I ran some business improvement workshops with a colleague. The workshops lasted two and a half days and with experience we recognized that by the afternoon of the first day delegates would be 'hitting the wall'. What we experienced was the frustration you feel when learning something new so that it's taking all of your cognitive brain power, which means you feel tired and frustrated. On the morning of the second day, usually after the team had 'bonded' in the bar, we noticed that some deep-level learning had happened overnight. We always started the morning session with a review of where they were at. As the group discussed what was happening it was apparent that they'd started to move into a different level of awareness. The reason we were able to make these observations is that we had created a process for the workshop – so that each time we ran it we became more certain what to expect. As the group facilitators (or coaches) we could relax knowing that the behaviours were normal outputs of the learning process and nothing unusual that we should potentially address. Having a process means that if you know what to expect it's much easier to release yourself from worrying about how you will intervene – and you can choose to think instead 'This is just the process working here.'

How to create a coaching process

There are a number of options to consider. Will you create this on your own? Will you work with a coach to help you? Will you work with a group of coaches? This doesn't have to be a solitary activity and in my experience benefits from having at least one other pair of eyes take a look. In the spirit of keeping things top level, to begin with let's start by getting clear that there are three simple characteristics of any process: beginning, middle, end! And there is one vital question: what do you want the process to produce as an output? There is also something that usually 'triggers' the process – this is the input. Let's listen to what that sounds like in coaching language:

- The client is experiencing dissatisfaction with their current situation or wishes to have/do/be more = Trigger.
- The coach and coachee meet to agree the coaching contract = start.
- The coach and coachee hold coaching sessions = middle.
- The coach and coachee come to the end of the coaching sessions = end.
- The coachee assesses the change in their situation = outcome.

There are typically three words in various forms that summarize the outcome of any process:

- to increase something;
- to decrease something;
- to maintain/stabilize something.

Coaches work hard with clients to state outcomes in positive language, and some of these outputs/outcomes might not sit easily with you – the fact remains that ultimately this is what the coaching process is looking to produce as an output. How you word that output is about the coaching techniques, behaviours and skills that you bring into the process. For example, if a coachee wishes to reduce their anxiety in giving presentations, that would be the process output. You might work with the coachee to create a positive outcome statement around being confident and what confidence looks feels and sounds like, and being able to present to any audience. So the process output, just to be clear, is what you are asking the process do. It's not about how you work with your coachees; it's about being clear and certain about the end point to help you create a meaningful process. Figure 4.2 gives an illustration of what that process might look like.

You now have a route map on which to develop your process further. At a top level a process typically has five or six key steps. That's not the whole story, because there will be other resources needed for the process to work and input that helps create the output. For those of you who are more sensing in their preferences I've created a process map for working with a group around personality type (Figure 4.3).

You can see in this diagram that input from another process is required as one of the start points for this process: the one-to-one feedback session. I've also illustrated how you might then drill down each process step to understand precisely what you'll be doing at that step (Figure 4.4). Once you have designed your group coaching process you can apply this process

FIGURE 4.2

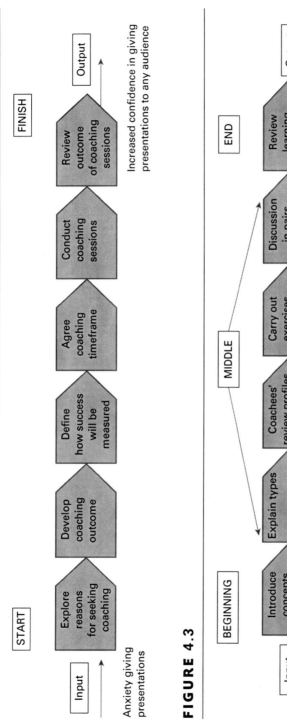

START

Input

Anxiety giving
presentations

Explore
reasons
for seeking
coaching

Develop
coaching
outcome

Define
how success
will be
measured

Agree
coaching
timeframe

Conduct
coaching
sessions

Review
outcome
of coaching
sessions

FINISH

Output

Increased confidence in giving
presentations to any audience

FIGURE 4.3

BEGINNING

Input

Personality
questionnaires

Introduce
concepts

Explain types

Coachees'
review profiles
Feedback notes

Carry out
exercises

MIDDLE

Discussion
in pairs

Review
learning
and next steps

END

Output

Understanding of type
and how their own
preference might affect
their behaviour and
choices

Feedback report
and notes

One-to-one
feedback
process

FIGURE 4.4

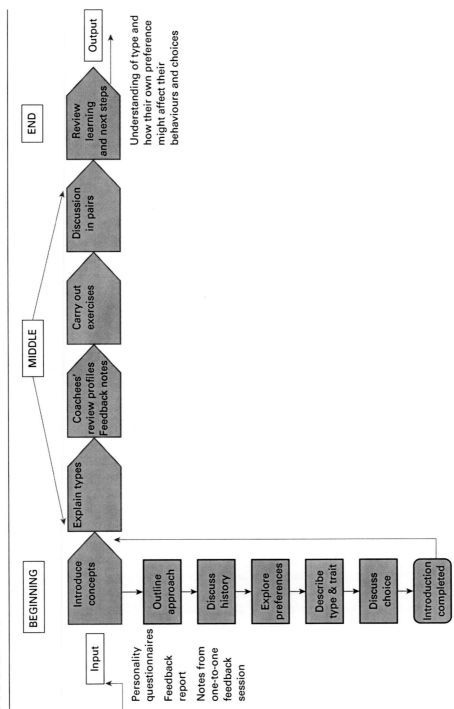

with other groups *and* you can adjust it as you learn from working with different groups. This forms your overarching process that helps you deliver your group coaching purpose. The interconnected nature of processes suggest that you might wish to think about designing your group coaching process to encompass the whole group coaching strategy: that is, from when you start to talk with a client through to disengagement with the client – or whenever your process starts and ends.

The process map is not the territory

So far we have looked at one aspect of your group coaching process – the part of the process that happens when you are in the room delivering a coaching session. As we've just seen this is not the whole story because that process sits within a wider set of processes and these, collected together, form your process map.

Here's an exercise you can do to help you see the landscape of your process map.

Exercise

Collect together some different coloured Post-it notes. Choose one colour for your top-level process and jot down the top-level steps, one step per Post-it. The aim is for five or six steps – if you have more than this, chunk up and save the remaining Post-its for use later on. Once you've identified your top-level processes think of all the things you do when you deliver group coaching. Keep writing one process per Post-it. Ideally each process should be described as 'Verb: Object'.

I have drawn up what this might look like to help illustrate the linkage of the processes (Figure 4.5). You'll see that three steps in my group coaching process link to my overall sales process and philosophy, and that three steps relate to my 'Deliver services' top-level process. This is only a high-level view of how everything you do in your coaching relates back to why and how you're doing it. How I sell my services and how I work as a group coach are interlinked – later on in this chapter I'll describe what I say to prospective clients to demonstrate why it's important to understand process congruence. Often the discord I've experienced when I've worked with groups in an organizational setting is because there is a lack of congruence between processes and policies that can create cognitive dissonance. Think of how your group coaching fits into the whole system so that you avoid working with the group in a disjointed way.

FIGURE 4.5

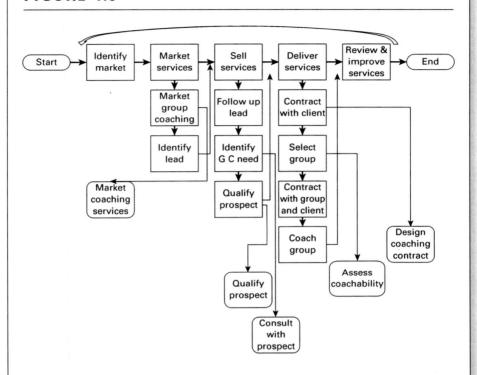

It is essential to take a systemic view (ie big picture) of how group coaching fits when you use it as part of your talent management strategy. It's even more important if there are a number of groups being coached simultaneously. For example, how the activities are coordinated might be something to consider within your wider process. Where there will be linkage and how it will fit with other talent development activities are questions and areas you must discuss at the engagement stage with your clients and coachees. After all, talent management is a systemic approach to attracting, developing, engaging and retaining talent in organizations and your coachees will have experienced firsthand what it's like to be part of that system. They will have subjective insights and experiences of how the system works in reality. Taking a strategic process view of where and how group coaching will benefit the wider system is part of the rationale for group coaching versus individual coaching. That by virtue of people working together in groups, the wider system will benefit and the synthesis of these groups working towards a bigger purpose will leverage the benefits we discussed earlier.

Keeping that big picture landscape inside your head sometimes helps with insights about what you experience within the group. Even better is to draw out on a map how you perceive the system, as this keeps it at the forefront of your mind and reminds you what other forces might be at play within the process. I have also found that when I lose sight of how everything fits together in my system it's more likely I'll make the wrong judgements about which actions to take. For me, the bigger landscape provides my moral compass and helps me make decisions about what feels right and what jars, and to understand that the group is part of a wider system and my experiences may just be feedback from that wider system.

The process is not a straightjacket

For those coaching colleagues who are no doubt shuddering at the mere mention of the word process, let's just remember that the process should never be a constraint to supporting the group rather a means to an end. This is the paradox I mentioned earlier – navigating process and behaviours. Sometimes the coach will 'stray' from the process to enable the group to develop and grow. This provides the coach with an opportunity to 'redesign' the process – to apply learning from its application and take on board feedback from the 'customers' of the process. All processes seek to serve 'customers', in whatever way you define customers. They are a transportation method to get the coachee from point A to B, which sometimes will mean going through X, Y and Z! The beauty of having a process is that it provides an opportunity to review and learn what went well and what didn't go so well. It also acts as a guidepost to bring you back to the outcome when you've meandered through the bush. Therefore, one of the outputs from all processes is the feedback and learning to help develop continuous process improvement.

What is the underlying core purpose of coaching? The answer is – personal development. This is both learning and the ability to apply the learning, self-knowledge and awareness beyond the scope of the coaching boundary. We are expecting that coachees will be able to apply what they've learnt during the coaching process to other contexts and situations so that they are able to achieve consistency in their results, lateral thinking and doing. Learning is about deliberate practice (Shenk, 2011) and deliberate practice is a process. How that process is designed will vary from individual to individual because we all have slightly different ways of learning. The art of designing a coaching process is to take account of that individuality and recognize that the 'process' does not drive the person, the person drives the process. So what works for one might not work for another.

You as the coach are responsible for creating a process that has inbuilt flexibility and allows scope for random activities and unconnected tasks as part of the learning. This means that you might have a process step that says: 'Encourage coachees to do, think, experience what feels right in the moment.' It will be apparent to those readers who are familiar with Myers Briggs Types that I have a judging preference – naturally I like to plan spontaneity! Actually in live group coaching sessions this preference is put to one side and just holding the space for the group becomes my modus operandi. Ultimately, beginning, middle and end is the guiding process and the aim is to know how you will create an environment in which you help the group reach a point where they can review, reflect, learn and apply what's just happened in the coaching session. That, above all else, is the most important thing. Keeping that 'beginner's mindset' and childlike curiosity by inviting your natural child to come out to play for a while and then waiting for your nurturing and structuring parent to lead you safely home. This then frees you to connect with the energy and emotion in the room. How you do it becomes the process – so long as the coachees don't feel 'processed' as a result! Hopefully this then reassures those coaches who like to work more free-flow with their groups. Build this free-flow activity into your process so that you can learn from it and replicate. The process only becomes a straightjacket if you design it as such.

Process behaviour

Building on this, let's revisit the notion of 'egoless' coaching and the implications for your coaching practice (ie behaviours). There are two sides to every coin and in this case those sides are process and behaviour. We have no way of knowing how a group will respond to a process until we apply it. Business process re-engineering encountered this challenge because even when processes are automated, human beings who interface with the process will find work-rounds if it makes their life easier. It is a fact of life that some people will always look to 'bend' the process to suit their own map of the world.

The contracting process

Clarifying expectations and gaining agreement about how you will work together is the starting point for any human relationship. This process is sometimes implied and sometimes declared. How well it serves the relationship is based on the degree of transparency and definition.

Dissatisfaction, grievances and disputes usually stem from an ill-defined contracting process where expectations are left unspoken and assumptions are made about what the other person will do and what they 'should' know (through some miraculous mythical universal law of 'how people should behave').

It is your job to get these expectations out into the open and gain agreement on what is ok and what is not ok at every step in your process. For example, an up-front contract with a new prospect about how you'll conduct the selling and buying process of your group coaching services. My up-front contract includes letting the prospect know, before we meet up, that it's ok to say 'No' if at the end of the meeting they don't feel my services are relevant for them. I also include a rough agenda of what we'll be discussing to make sure we both know what's included in the scope of the meeting. I ask them to confirm that's what they're expecting and/or change anything. That way we'll all enter the meeting at least with a higher degree of certainty of what to expect. At the end of the meeting I remind them of the agreement we made up front at the beginning of the meeting about it being ok for them to say 'Yes' or 'No'. I ask them if it's a 'Yes' or a 'No'. Anything other than a 'Yes' or 'No' is usually a 'No'! People like to be liked and if I hear or sense any equivocation I will declare that I am interpreting it as a 'No'.

Let's take a pause here and review what you've just read. What did you experience inside as you read that last paragraph? What did the voice in your head say? Where did it come from? Was it an emotional response or a logical response? If logical, what might your unconscious mind really be saying to you? I suspect that you will have had an emotional response to the paragraph because it's not the sort of behaviour we typically expect in the sales dance, is it? After all, surely you want the prospect to say yes and you do everything in your power to convince them that they should buy your services. Here's the rub – if you become so attached to that outcome, it's likely that your ego is driving the conversation. The consequences of that might be you 'push' the prospect in the opposite direction, or they buy from you because you've convinced them – rather than them convincing themselves. If the latter, you will have potentially created an expectation that you then might not be able to meet. And if that voice is saying, 'Of course I'd be able to meet their expectations', ask yourself – how do you know?

So why have I taken you down a side alley when talking about contracting in group coaching? Contracting in the group coaching sessions follows the same principles as in any type of human interaction: ensure that the internal psychological process is as much in the open as possible. This means both having a process and applying behaviours – what you'll do and how you'll do it – to create the space for people to feel safe to open up about what's really in their mind as they enter the room for their group coaching session. My process step is: contract with the group. I have various tools, techniques and methods that I use to do this. And sometimes I'll arrive at the group session with something prepared that I then discard if I sense that the group is less likely to respond well to that particular approach. For me this is an internal, somatic process that, when I am truly mindful, means I tap into the intuitive data my senses are giving me. For example, how I am responding internally to the energy in the room. What have I noticed about the way people are speaking and interacting as they come through the door?

One experience I had was delivering a training session as opposed to pure group coaching. I arrived in plenty of time and prepared the room in the way I normally do. I wasn't particularly happy with the room as it was a bit pokey and impersonal – I noticed my emotional response to the environment, which I put to one side. As people started to arrive I noticed they were having aside conversations with each other and from their tone of voice, pace and the actual things they were discussing I was picking up a sense that all was not well. It was my 'spider sense' alerting me to something happening in the wider context that was likely to impact receptiveness for the task at hand. As I started the session, using the format of the training run, I realized that the sensory data I had experienced was being confirmed by the reality of what they were now saying to me. In that moment I took a decision to adopt a coaching approach rather than slavishly follow the format for the introductory session. I gave the group permission to tell me what was going on and put a boundary around it by saying: 'We'll spend time getting this out in the open and then once it's out there you can decide what you want to do with it. Then we'll imagine that it's put into a box and left outside the room so that we can continue with the training. Is everyone ok with that?' Sure enough everyone was ok with that and we were able to get all the emotional stuff out there and had a plan for what they would do with it after the session.

It was a challenging experience for me as the 'trainer turned group coach' because I was also having an emotional response to the situation. I'd been given a task and was balancing the need to deliver the task for the paying client and at the same time deliver the outcome that the delegates wanted. 'Coaching tightrope walking' is the name I'll use for this, because looking down at how I was feeling was akin to a severe case of vertigo. It was crucial to put aside my needs and ego to allow the group to move forward from this point since if I'd just continued with my agenda the session would not have worked anyway. I hopefully created a space for them to purge the emotion so that they could do something positive with it and also benefit from the content of the course.

Letting go of ego means you are free to choose a response based on what you're experiencing in the moment. When I teach coaching skills I always spend a long time on the contracting process, explaining to the delegates what I'm doing and why. It's about how 'we' will work together and what will be covered, how people are feeling at the start of the process and how you'll introduce each subsequent coaching session. For example, in the contracting process I use flipcharts and Post-its. I usually start a discussion with a 'What's in your mind?' type question and after we've discussed this I ask them to summarize on Post-its or write directly on the flipcharts. We then move into the 'ground rules' – how we'll work together which I then roll up at the end of the session and keep ready to revisit at each subsequent session. I have also used playing cards, for this I stick a blank label on the back of each card so that coachees can write on them. I ask them what cards they'd like to 'get on the table' and ask them to write these on the blank labels on the back of the playing cards, one thought per card. We stick these cards on a piece of flipchart paper ready to use again. There are many ways to get the psychological contract out in the open – more ideas will come later in the chapter on tools and sharing techniques from other group coaches. The essential ingredients are declaring expectations to get them out in the open and agreeing how all of you will work together through any challenges and potential obstacles. I am sometimes surprised, though not often, by things that people bring to this part of the coaching; I have learnt that it is more productive the less emotionally attached I am to doing the 'right process' and the more engaged I am with a process that's right for the group.

The psychodynamics within group coaching are different from those in one-to-one coaching primarily because of numbers. It is much easier to hold the space for one person than it is for many. Each individual within the group will bring their own expectations and needs that will co-exist with the group's expectations and needs. The group in this sense becomes a living, breathing entity and is the manifestation of the collective energy of the individuals. Balancing the needs and expectations of the individual with those of the group is why the contracting process is so important. This be-comes your anchor point for challenging disruptive or unhelpful behaviours and reinforcing learning through adherence to what the group has agreed. It's also a sanity check for you as the coach and enables you to do some self-coaching when you experience behaviours in the group that don't make sense. Understanding what goes on beneath the surface is one of the key skills that a coach can bring to the group and is perhaps one of the most challenging to master. Coaching is not an exact science and the contracting process requires a significant amount of self-confidence from the coach so that they can let go of their ego and retain an adult-to-adult perspective. The process itself is simple, but that doesn't mean it's always easy.

Co-creating the group coaching process

Co-creation lies at the heart of egoless coaching since the coach truly shares responsibility and creativity with the group. Looking back at the premise for this book – that group coaching is a means to leverage and optimize talent through groups – co-creating the group coaching process is the most practical way to achieve this aspirational goal. For most coaches this will be 'common sense' – the one-to-one coaching relationship is that of equals and works best when there is a strong sense of co-creation. In a group setting this emergent activity has to be thought through to work well so that you take account of the group dynamics. This is where I rely on my simple 'beginning, middle, end' model. I spend a lot of time thinking about how I will set the scene for the session and help create the space for the group so that they feel free to release ideas, thoughts and feelings to shape the session. This includes coaching them to think about how they will work with the space. I have usually prepared a default ending for the session, which I may or may not use depending on the content of the session the group designs. The essential ingredients for the ending to the session will usually be around learning and value. How that is played out emerges and evolves as the session develops.

Co-creating the process for the session in this way requires a 'letting go' of the process reins and a firm grip of coaching skills. How well it works is influenced by the energy of the coach to encourage the group and demonstrate freedom for everyone to own the process. A congruent coach who is completely comfortable in their own skin and willing to take calculated risks to facilitate the group's development will help create an environment for experimentation. Some groups balk at the challenge and want the coach to be responsible for their learning. For me this is another opportunity to question the group about their mindset and what might really be going on for them in admitting this. All groups differ according to the makeup of the individuals and their collective experiences and assumptions about the context in which the coaching is happening. How the group responds is another piece of data for the coach and might indicate the maturity of the group, and this is always an opportunity for the coach to reflect back to the group for further learning.

Co-creating the process is another opportunity to help the group learn techniques they can apply away from the coaching. After all, if you have the ability to help others create a process for learning then how might this improve their relationships with others? At the beginning of this chapter we looked at how the realization of strategy is through process, which on the surface probably sounds less than scintillating; after all, as coaches we learn an implicit presupposition that anything to do with coaching must be 'life-changing'. The reality is that only through an understanding of your own process can you help others learn and spark their creative juices so that they are able to tap into dormant or hidden depths. Sometimes, the prosaic can be catalytic, since talent is the realization of potential capability into reality through a process of deliberate practice. Having a strategy and developing processes are only the start – where they take you is down to you as the coach. It's ultimately about learning and application through action – co-creation is both a process and a meta-process for doing that, since the coachees experience both personal development and, by participating in the co-creation process, help others to have the same experience. In addition, this process can continue long after the coaching finishes and hopefully become self-perpetuating.

The overarching strategy for group coaching determines how you will work with groups. It provides the characteristics for how coachees are likely to experience the coaching and elevates it from being a one-time activity to self-perpetuating learning. In an organizational setting, using your group coaching strategy as an integrated tool within the wider talent management system means that you create a systemic view of talent management and ensure continuous improvement as part of the organizational growth experience. Optimizing collective talent is partly about how well the group coaching process manifests synthesis: that the grouping of individuals creates something new. For individual clients, this is likely to be about developing their talents so that they are better equipped to work within their own business and social systems. For organizations, it's about ensuring that your group coaching process works within the wider organizational system. In short, your group coaching processes should be both logical and consciously interrelated with your client's and coachees' system. In the next chapter I give you some ideas for creating your own blueprints.

KEY POINTS

- A strategy is an overarching decisive course of action that will lead you to your objective. It's a plan for realizing your coaching purpose.

- A process is a collection of related tasks that through a series of steps act on input to create output. All coaching models and tools use a process if they are to assist continuous learning and development.

- Your group coaching process provides a means to help you:

  - create a flow of sequential steps;

  - determine and sequence critical steps in that flow;

  - identify the most important outcomes of the activities;

  - provide a repeatable model you can use, adapt and improve.

- Mapping out your total coaching processes end to end enables you to see where links occur and what part of your process might have an unintended consequence.

- Contracting is essential for your process to fly. Behaviours will determine how well your process works, and setting the scene for expectations, needs and wants each and every time you meet provides the space for learning and insight.

- Co-creating the coaching process is an optimal learning and self-development vehicle and is the mainstay of egoless coaching.

05

Group coaching blueprint

A group coaching process is the means by which the group coaching blueprint comes to life. We've already explored purpose and direction, so devising a blueprint breathes life into that purpose. In simple terms a blueprint is a plan, reference or guide for what you do. In a sense it's an expanded form of the tick list we talked about earlier, but with the added benefit of forming your process. In this chapter I share my blueprint process, which I've used many times and adapted to the needs of the group and the context. There is no right or wrong process, only what works for you and the group. I like to keep things simple and straightforward – my preference is for the big picture. At the beginning of our journey together I emphasized the importance of adopting a beginner's mindset, and if you are to develop group coaching skills this approach will serve you well. Having a blueprint is a great starting point, and sometimes you will prepare a process to share with the group and they will want to do something different. Understanding what works for you and the group is part of the learning cycle. Take a Darwinian approach to developing your blueprint:

The system with the greatest flexibility has the greatest chance of success.

Prime directive

It is a universal truth that all great things have a three-letter acronym! And this is especially true in organizations. My three-letter acronym is TLC, which is based on my overriding prime directive in coaching and facilitation, which is: first do no harm! The first step to designing a group coaching blueprint starts with articulating a prime directive. My prime directive stems from my purpose:

To help people connect with others with their head, heart and inner strength – otherwise known as spirit – so that they have access to the capacity to grow and develop together. Anyone can be great given the right environment, support, process and opportunity to practise.

In ensuring that I first do no harm I am helping to create an environment in which my coachees are supported to grow and develop together. This means I treat each group coaching assignment with care and recognize that as soon as I walk in the room I have made a difference. We established earlier the principle of 'authority', and the very act of being there as the coach means you will influence the dynamic in the room – whether consciously or not. Think about this for a minute – if you weren't in the room what would happen with that group of people? Your very presence creates a different dynamic within the group, a different set of expectations. It is no accident that I chose the acronym TLC – it unconsciously reminds me that I have to take care of both the group and myself to ensure that I can create a safe space for people to explore and grow. In fact, this is my prime directive in everything I do, whether it's one-to-one coaching, consultancy, training, facilitation or presenting. It's another example of being mindful of how we affect others without realizing it. That's not to say you as the group coach can 'control' how people feel and perceive – that is their response-ability. What you can do is help control for 'interference' that might get in the way of the group having a meaningful and useful coaching experience.

Exercise

A prime directive is something that acts as a guide to making decisions around your core purpose and inspires how you behave. Spend a few minutes bringing to life your own prime directive. Think back to a time when you were totally congruent with your purpose. What were you doing, saying and feeling in that moment? What was it like? Maybe you could draw an image that represents it? What is the metaphor for your prime directive? Really tap into your values and beliefs. What image, word, thought or even smell might you use to create an anchor so that you can feel secure in your prime directive. What might your acronym be? And remember three-letter acronyms are popular because they're easy to remember! So keep it short and sweet.

TLC for group coaching

Having explored your prime directive, here's my blueprint, or reference point, for coaching groups: Task – Limit – Climate. The mind can only keep a small amount of data in the energy hungry pre-frontal cortex (Rock, 2009). It can sometimes be challenging to keep on track whilst in the flow of coaching, particularly where you are working with either a challenging group or situation. Having a simple point of reference keeps you grounded and develops confidence in your process. 'Trusting the process' first means having a process to trust and this easy-to-remember blueprint means you can apply it to every stage of the process.

Task

There is always a task to be performed – otherwise why are you there? We can sometimes ascribe negative connotations to the word 'task', but in reality without a task to be performed there is no reason for the group coaching. In a positive way, the task is really a lower form of the purpose and answers the 'reason why'. Why is that particular group looking for coaching? Why is that particular individual in the group seeking group coaching? As the coach you are there to help resolve or solve two tasks:

- The outcome task. This is what the group and the client sponsor wants to achieve from the group coaching. This is what they expect will be different by the end of the coaching. It's how they'll measure 'success'.

- The group coaching task. This is about how you as the coach help the group learn and grow together. It's about what opportunities, experiences and process you create to increase learning and enable their talents to shine.

Getting clear about these tasks before you start coaching the group helps keep you on track about your purpose. Here's a thought – would it be useful to share this insight with the group before you start the coaching? If you were to share this with the group – that this is your group coaching beacon – asking them what they think, feel and see about this might be a great way of understanding what's happening at a deeper level as they enter the group coaching relationship.

Limits

The limits and limitations are 'interference' that might get in the way of the coaching. Some of them can be mitigated and others are reality factors that have to be managed. For instance, the time you have available during the coaching session is a given reality. How you manage that time is down to your skill as the coach and the discipline of the group. The list below is the limits and limitations I have experienced:

- the time you and the group have available;
- the knowledge of the people in the room – both your knowledge and knowledge of each other;
- the facilities you have in which to conduct the coaching;
- the will of the group to work on the task;
- the will of the group to be coached;
- your beliefs;
- your values;
- your personality type;
- the personality type of the people within the group;
- the beliefs of the people in the group;
- the values of the individuals within the group.

Exercise

This is a quick exercise to help you outline some of the limits that might be present in your group coaching. What other limits have you experienced? What limits might you experience?

1 Quickly write down your own list of limits. Keep this list free from judgement and write freely. Really tap into your unconscious mind. Sometimes it helps to move to a different room, or different seat. If you've already done a lot of group coaching, re-visit those experiences and re-live them so that you can see, hear and experience the limits that you experienced in that moment.

2 Look at your list and move to a different chair or room to do this next step. Really tap into your judgement-free brain and allow yourself to create lots of ways of mitigating those limits. If you're using words, write quickly. If you're drawing images, draw quickly. Or perhaps you want to record your thoughts –

if so, keep the voice steady and flowing. How many different ways can you create to mitigate those limits?

3   This final step is about reframing the limits you came up with at Step 1. How might you reframe some of these limits to make them positive? Take each limit and rephrase the sentence into a positive statement. Think about the positive intent behind the limit. For example, a positive intent of a time limit is to keep the group focused and clear on their outcome.

This simple exercise could be used with a group starting out their group coaching journey. As part of the contracting process you could ask them what limits or limitations might be present. And at the end of each step, have a discussion before moving to the next step. Or you could ask them to work in pairs on Step 2. Be creative about how you use the exercise – what you're looking for is an opportunity to get out into the open the underlying expectations about limits. The final step, reframing, is part of the coaching process since it helps you and the group learn that if you approach an obstacle as an opportunity for learning then the negative energy dissipates. It taps into that inherent capacity to grow by practising a different thinking pattern. It's also a great way to provide material for other sessions. When you and the group encounter a challenging dynamic, revisiting some of the limitations you've outlined provides a door to insights. 'Remembering the work we did around limitations, what might this [what we're experiencing at the moment] really be about?'

Climate

This is the one that I suspect probably creates the fear element for anyone moving into group coaching. I personally find it the most fascinating, challenging and interesting. I guess it's all about perspectives. Essentially, if you're comfortable in your own skin then no matter what happens you'll see it as an opportunity for personal development and growth. So what do we mean by climate?

- The group dynamics.

- The context in which the group have come together, ie any politics.

- Their personal stories that they bring to the group, which might manifest as either positive or negative.

- The physical climate in the room, for example heat, light, space, noise – never underestimate the impact this can have! Remember, in Maslow's hierarchy of needs environment is one of the foundation needs.

TLC is easy to remember and keeps me grounded in my prime directive and purpose. It's the first blueprint in my group coaching toolkit.

Here's one we prepared earlier

A picture paints a thousand words, and to help create your own blueprint I have drawn some process flows to stimulate your thinking. I have included some core questions alongside to help guide you through. The content of each process step will be determined by you and your coachees. If you are starting on your journey this may be an evolutionary process as you gain experience of what works and what doesn't work so well. If you've been group coaching for a while, it might be interesting to see another process and compare this with your own. Clearly our own personal preferences influence the process we use – even those coaches who claim not to have a process will invariably have one. A process is a habit or routine that you default to, so just becoming aware of this will make you notice what you do as a matter of course. If you are an online group coach, you will probably have a process that takes account of the inherent challenges of coaching people remotely and in geographically dispersed locations. Group coaching online requires a different process because you've added in technology and changed the dynamics of how the 'group' will interact. Starting with a blueprint on which to build the different scenarios means that you're not starting from scratch each and every time you work with a group – regardless of the method.

TLC provides a system blueprint in which the overall group coaching process operates. There are three key steps in my process, simply because it's easier for me to remember (Figure 5.1). You will see later that the process becomes more sophisticated the deeper we go. So in coaching terms I have chunked up my process to the three core steps. The output of my process flows into three other processes: the group coaching process for learning and updates, the customer satisfaction process – because I want to know what customers like and value – and finally, there is the marketing process. Preparing the coaching relationship might also be a process to consider, depending on what comes out of the feedback and evaluation. There are probably other processes that feed from the overall group coaching process but I have deliberately kept it short and sweet so that you have a starter for 10 to create your own blueprint. In an organization setting I would expect to see a direct link from the steps in my process to the client's talent management process. The data gained from the group coaching experience will form

FIGURE 5.1

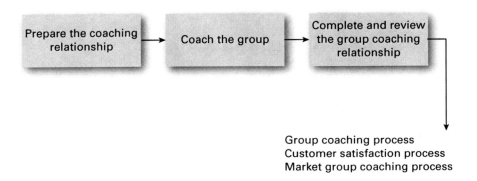

input for their talent management activities – particularly if they are using group coaching as an overt means to develop talent.

The first detailed step in my overall group coaching process is creating the coaching relationship. There are many great tools in *50 Top Tools For Coaching* about how to contract with clients and coachees, and these can easily be adapted to work with groups. I will include my own adapted version of some of these in the chapter on 'Discovering the right tools'. In Figure 5.2 you will see that I have a process step that assesses coachability.

Here are some questions and points for you to consider in preparing the coaching relationship:

- Outcomes – speak to all coachees, one-to-one conversations.
- Coachees – who, where, what types, how many?
- Is there a minimum and maximum for group size?
- Are you able to pre-qualify for coachability?
- Return on investment/how they will value coaching – tangible or intangible? How will it be measured?
- Contracting:
  - Client sponsor (if there is one). What will you agree between you about how you will behave? Who will own what?
  - Coachees. Will you have an individual and group contract? How will you manage overlap or conflicting needs/wants/expectations from the coaching?
- Explore boundaries – what is ok and not ok?
- How do you feel about coaching this group of people?
- What might get in the way of/help the coaching?

FIGURE 5.2

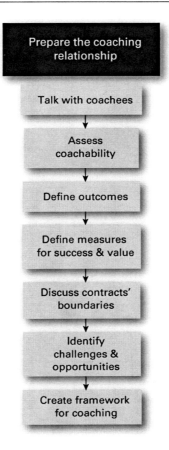

For me, assessing coachability is an important step even where you are working with organizations. There are some individuals for whom coaching either isn't suitable (because they require another type of intervention such as training, mentoring, counselling etc) or who just don't want to work with a coach and are not likely to implement any actions and change behaviours. My upfront contract with the client covers this so that there is an expectation that not everyone will qualify. This is a vital process step as groundwork for managing a positive group dynamic. This is impossible if you are starting from a position where group coaching is not the best intervention or there is resistance to the process. Setting the groundwork for the coaching itself and clarity about expectations from all sides is the outcome. Promising the earth and delivering nothing will result in dissatisfaction for everyone involved. It is at this stage that the contracting process begins – at an individual level.

The contracting process with the group is at the next step. Learning how to work together with differing expectations is part of the trick of being successful in any organization or relationship. It presents the group with their first lesson in developing interpersonal skills and behaviours that are directly transferable to work and life generally. You will see that I have noted down some questions to think about and use at the different steps in the process.

Time out exercise

Spend a few minutes allowing your mind to run free and absorb what you've just read:

- What do you take from this?
- Does this make sense?
- How do you feel about what you've just read?
- Do you agree or disagree?
- Which parts strike a chord and sound ok?
- Which parts jarred?
- Do you already have a blueprint that you follow?
- Where did this come from?
- How often do you look at it?
- What have you updated and changed and what have you kept the same?
- Why is that?

Coaching the group is where the rubber hits the road and this is where I engage my beginning, middle, end process (Figure 5.3). I have outlined some of the things at each of these stages, including a decision point for you and the group around which process you will be using.

Here are some questions and points for you to consider:

- Structure – loose/fixed/mixture? Are the outcomes clear? Is the purpose clear?
- How do the coachees define success for the coaching?
- What will you agree up front?
- Do they want to set an overall plan for the coaching sessions?
- Interventions – will you use an overarching model? What tools and techniques will help?

FIGURE 5.3

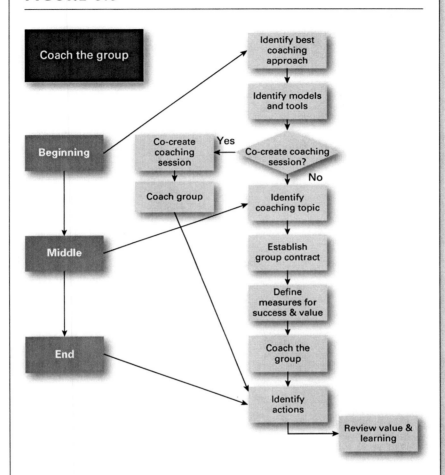

- What might you have to adapt in your style?

- What approach will you take as the coach?

- How are you going to measure success as the coach? And how will the participants measure success?

- How will you work with the group?

- What action(s) will people commit to? How will you know they are committed?

- What have people valued and learnt?

- What will be covered at the next meeting?

- What feedback will you solicit at the end of the session and over the course of the coaching?

Consider also whether or not you will be co-creating the process for the session and other sessions or will follow your own process. If you are co-creating the session, I have demonstrated how I loop this back into my process at the end. This is a personal choice and is not always what happens, particularly if the group decide their own method of evaluating the session as part of the process they've co-created. Where I do verge towards 'directive coaching' is at the 'taking action' step because this is an important stage in the learning process. Simply talking something through will not help change behaviour patterns – doing something will. There is evidence to suggest that mentally rehearsing and practising something will ultimately effect change in behaviour (Doidge, 2008; Shenk, 2011). So taking action doesn't always manifest in the material world, but it does have to be purposeful and repeated. For example, learning to play the piano in the mind can be as effective as learning to play it for real provided learners experience the keys and movement in their mental rehearsal *as if* they were rehearsing on the physical keyboard. Talking and thinking about topics and then not revisiting them or not practising different mental habits outside the coaching is not action in my books!

A question I learnt many years ago – How will you know? – is a key part of the actions review in the process. How will you know that you've made progress? What actions will you take and how will you review the results? If you're not going to take action, how will you leverage the benefit from the coaching session today? This is about engaging the group in the learning process and stimulating them to think through how they'll apply the learning. Even if they don't propose direct actions, asking them to think through how they'll leverage the benefits from the coaching stimulates learning and brings to their conscious minds what they've learnt and where it adds value. The conscious mind, as we've established, is energy hungry and moves through events and experiences quickly, without always capitalizing on the learning. The purpose of coaching is to bring the 'out of awareness part' of the mind to the fore so that we become consciously aware of what we are learning in order to apply it to other scenarios and continuously add to it. In talent management terms, this is about developing latent capacity and turning it into talents.

The next step is to review the overall process and outcomes once the coaching has been completed so that the total experience can be evaluated, and lessons learned and fed into other processes. It's the culmination of the group coaching purpose since this is when you as the coach know whether you've met your overall coaching strategy and the client and coachees are able to assess how it was for them. In my process at Figure 5.4 I have a decision because not all group coaching has an overall sponsor – particularly where you are running it as an open group for individual members of the public to join.

Here are some questions and points for you to consider:

- Evaluation – how will the coaching be evaluated by the coachees and the client sponsor (if there is one)?

FIGURE 5.4

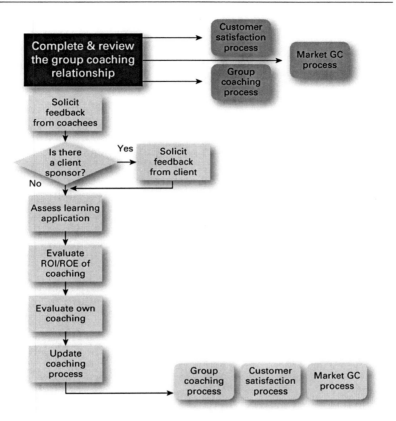

- Checking back on return on investment/expectation – are you able to measure and have you measured?

- Feedback – what feedback will you solicit and from whom?

- Did the coaching achieve the outcome? How do you know?

- Are they applying learning? What has happened since? What help could you provide in assisting with this?

- What have you learned about your group coaching that you could build on/do differently?

An important part of this process step is the evaluation of your own coaching. This is about taking an honest 'drains up' perspective on how well you worked with the group, what you learnt about your coaching style, how you felt about the coaching experience, what surprised you, what challenged you and how well it measured up against your definition of 'success'.

GROW as a process

The purpose of this book is to provide you with practical tools and techniques you can use and apply – there is a coaching strategy to the way the book is written and a process for you to follow. In outlining my blueprint of group coaching I have attempted to give you a framework on which you can develop your own blueprint – a 'straw man' for you to pick apart and create something even better. A working knowledge of processes gives you the capability to create and be innovative with basic coaching models and apply them to group coaching. With that in mind, let's explore how we can use a well-known coaching model and apply it to a group coaching process.

The GROW model is one of the most often used models in coaching: Goal, Reality, Options, and Wrap up or Will. So at a simple level this is a four-step process – or is it? Looking back at the simple definition of a process it is clear that GROW is a related set of tasks with each step creating an output, and it is repeatable. The fact is that coachees are not always ready to launch straight in at the goal step – they want to 'download', as I call it, their thoughts to help them work out what they want. I was reminded of this recently when I worked with a group of coaches. I made a massive assumption that I could skip certain steps in the process because I was working with coaches. I soon realized that even though at a cognitive level coaches understand the coaching process, they're still human beings. The importance of holding the space to enable the group to be physically and mentally present in the room cannot be overstated. So let's look at how GROW might be represented as a process (Figure 5.5).

As you will see, there is more than one direction for the flow because coachees may well go back and forth in their thinking/experience of the coaching. GROW is probably too complex to represent as a simple flow and is probably more like a whole series of iterative steps, as in Figure 5.6.

As an aside, in his book on the brain and how it works David Rock (2009) explains that the prefrontal cortex, the part of the brain responsible for imagining or picturing something, is extremely energy hungry. 'Picturing something you have not yet seen is going to take a lot of energy and effort.' Asking a group to picture their goal may well send their brains into free-fall because they don't have a reference point for 'imagining' what that something is that can be achieved. And it is likely that the coachees will already have used up a lot of brain power before they arrive at the coaching session. This is useful information for the coach since it provides input for what the first 'activity' of the session could be – something that helps

FIGURE 5.5

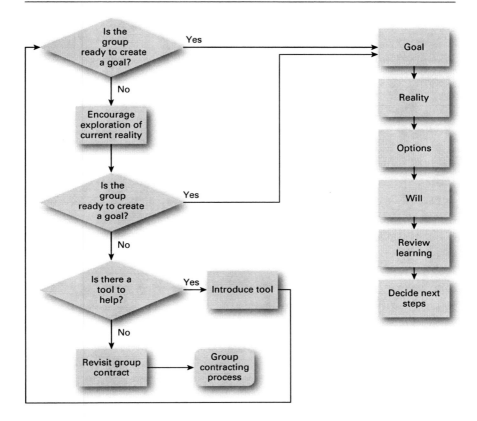

FIGURE 5.6

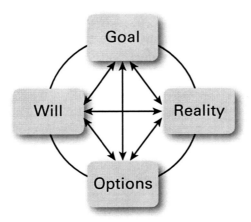

re-energize the coachees' brain. And for the goal setting, perhaps some reference points to support and ignite the 'imagining' process of the brain. For example, magazine images, PowerPoint images projected onto a screen, storytelling at the beginning of the session, are all useful resources. The coach can use any tool or technique in their armoury that allows the brain to work less and so conserves energy.

Group coaching as growth

In their paper outlining how the GROW model can be adapted to a group setting, Brown and Grant (2010) explore the nature of group coaching compared with individual coaching and create two steps in the process to turn GROW into GROUP – the U is for understanding others and the P is for performing. This a neat way of encompassing group dynamics in the coaching process and keeping the spirit of GROW alive. After all, the will and commitment to take action starts with understanding how we impact and interact with others in addition to practising what we've learnt. Their model also illustrates the importance of the coach's skill in synthesizing group and individual learning. Using GROW with groups means getting creative about the process, not blindly following questions or assuming that one step flows from another. If you decide to adapt GROW, then consider how you will include the exploration of intra and interpersonal dynamics. How will you ensure that the learning process is incorporated into the elements of GROW? How will you work with the model so that the group can revisit the different stages and be free to experience and think in a 'disconnected' stream? The GROW model is not a four-step process but, with imagination, can become a powerful stepping-off point to a rich resource for the group coach.

Dweck (2006) created the phrase 'growth mindset' and the concept of growth inherent in the GROW model is one of the reasons I particularly like the GROW acronym. It has the powerful concept at its core of increasing something, of developing from the inside out. The implied belief that each of us has the capacity to develop beyond our current state is powerful – whether we choose to tap into that capacity is a matter of choice. The GROW model returns me once again to my coaching purpose. How I work with it will be determined by the context, the group and both my and the group's current reality. In effect the GROW model provides me with a meta-process for coaching the group. The ever-present questions in my unconscious mind, out of awareness but always within reach, are:

- What's the outcome – for me? For the group?
- Where is the group at this moment in time?
- Where am I now?
- What options and resources do I have available to me to help the group?
- What options and resources does the group have available to help them?
- How willing am I to take these options?
- How willing is the group to take these options?
- Where is there resistance?
- Where is there energy to move forward?

It reminds me that I can work only with the current reality and that if I operate with an open mind, acknowledging my own willingness to commit to work with the group, then I will be satisfying my purpose.

Developing your own blueprint

There is no one right way to work with a group; there is only one way that is right for that particular group. In creating your own blueprint, remember to build in flexibility since that is the key to providing the best opportunity for a group to learn and grow. Having explored what is a process, the elements of my blueprint and some of the insights from others, kick back your shoes and take a few minutes to allow your mind to explore what all of this means for you. If you're already experienced in group coaching, no doubt you have a ready-made blueprint up your sleeve. Those of you new to the experience might have some ideas but nothing really concrete. And even if you do have a blueprint that has served you well you might wish to reinvent or completely revolutionize that blueprint. The following is an idea to generate some new thoughts and feelings about your blueprint – experiment with it, setting aside any reservations, and then when you've finished review what you've learnt and the insights you've gained. Even if those insights are: I'll stick with what I'm doing!

Exercise

Before you start this exercise, remembering what we know about the prefrontal cortex, make sure that you've had a glass of water and something to eat – preferably something healthy. And if it helps, spend a few minutes just letting your mind wander so that you're fully energized to do some imagining.

1 Big thinking is helped by big pictures, so take several pieces of flipchart paper and stick them edge to edge so that you create a huge piece of blank paper. Decide whether you wish to stick it on a wall with masking tape or sticky tac, or prefer to place it on the floor so you can walk through your creation. Go with your first intuitive response on this one. I quite like the idea of placing it on the floor so that I can experience the journey as I create it.

2 Draw a road on the paper – make it big and create twists and turns in the road to bring it to life. You might even consider using a printout of a map and using a real road to represent your group coaching blueprint.

3 Collect magazine images, textiles, anything that will help make the journey come alive; choose images that make sense for you to represent the different stops along the way. For example, one of my images would be a coffee shop.

4 Using masking tape or sticky tac, place the images on your road. The coffee shop for me would be one of the first stops on my road.

5 Use a story to create the journey – anything that helps bring to life the group coaching blueprint and make it real.

One of the reasons for placing the paper on the floor is that you could even use a child's toy car to physically drive along the road to experience the different stops. If something is in the wrong place, move it to the right place in the road. By the way, the image of the coffee shop symbolizes the coming together of the group when you first meet. I might also have a picture of a dove to represent the contracting process and possibly a bank to represent the collection point for the coachees' outcomes – to keep them safe. The key is to make it fun and really dig deep into your own unconscious mind, using images to help uncover what's really important for you in your blueprint and what that means for you and your coachees.

You could also use this approach to help your coachees work together on creating their group coaching blueprint. This provides a rich resource to discover what's behind the story for the coachees and to elicit roadblocks and roadworks that might crop up in the coaching journey.

How did you find this exercise? If you had blueprint already, will you stick with it? If you didn't, what insights did you uncover? Did you do the exercise? Did it remind you of being back at primary school? If so, that's great! Developing your own blueprint for group coaching does not mean that it has to look like a boring process flow! Creating a blueprint that works for you is the key to enabling you to coach the group from a position of self-trust and trust in the process. The essential thing is that you create something that will work for you and has enough process in there so that you can learn and master it.

Keeping a beginner's mind

There are many stories about great inventors having eureka moments – often when they allow their minds to run free, like Archimedes taking a bath. Some of my most creative ideas have emerged as I've cleaned my teeth. In fact, I usually have my best insights when I'm doing something mundane like washing up or cooking. It's all about giving the brain 'time out' from the constant energy drain we subject it to with critical thinking. When we apply critical reasoning we lose our natural child-like curiosity, which prevents us from truly learning and exploring the wonders of 'not knowing' something. Can you remember the first time you learnt how to ride a bike or found out a fact that blew your mind. Exploration is one of the key tenets of coaching and a child-like curiosity frees us from the 'serious adult' syndrome that is required of us in the normal scheme of things. The group coaching experience is an opportunity to liberate the mind from the constraints of social norms and expectations. How often are you allowed to give your creativity free rein in a work environment? There are usually set parameters about what you can and can't do to 'innovate' in the work environment. The group coaching experience is about keeping a beginner's mindset, which means creating a space for you and your coachees to get comfortable with being uncomfortable. Once you have developed a group coaching blueprint, remember to keep it fresh. Incorporate opportunities to take yourself out of your comfort zone so that you experience what it's like to 'not know'. Tapping into that resource of 'not knowing' means that you as the coach are free to explore with your coachees and experience the learning process together. Sometimes we coaches can try too hard to be the perfect exemplar of cool and calm. Life, as we know, isn't always like that, and allowing yourself that possibility of child-like curiosity and learning frees up your coachees to follow suit.

For me it would be the importance of preparation, especially with the online stuff. But also so important with the face-to-face work as well – so you're personally prepared so that you are in the right space and you've got your presence. It's almost as though the more you can prepare beforehand, or for me anyway, the easier it then becomes to just go with the flow once the session starts. If I'm poorly prepared I'll be finding myself looking for a structure or model to cling onto in desperation because I haven't got the confidence to just go with what's happening.

Angela Dunbar, master clean language and emergent knowledge coach

The experience of coaching a group of coaches taught me two key lessons:

- Contract with the group up front around willingness for both you and them to experiment and take risks so that you learn together.
- Be willing to allow the coach to let go of perfection.

In other words, the coach won't always get it right, but provided everyone learns something from the experience that's fine. Co-creating the group coaching experience means both you and the coachees taking responsibility for holding a beginner's mindset. Your group coaching blueprint will keep you anchored and support your own development as a group coach so that you can provide an opportunity for the group to go out of their comfort zone.

KEY POINTS

- There is no right or wrong group coaching blueprint – only a blueprint that works for you and the group.

- A prime directive that stems from your group coaching purpose provides congruence and helps remind you what behaviours will help.

- Creating an overall blueprint system from which your coaching process operates helps keep you grounded and capable of coping with any situation.

- Your overall blueprint provides a reference point for what you do, how you'll do it and why that's important. It also needs to feed into your client's process so that you can both realize your outcomes.

- GROW is really a model. It can be turned into a group coaching process provided it takes account of how we learn and how we relate and interact with others. It's iterative and not necessarily sequential.

- Group coaching is about growth, which necessitates a beginner's mindset and willingness to step out of your comfort zone. It's about modelling for your coachees a child-like curiosity and experimental approach to learning.

- Reframing your blueprint can sometimes provide an opportunity to do something different. Flexibility is important in the design and application of any blueprint.

06 Group dynamics and the group directive

One of the most fascinating aspects of human behaviour is how we act in a group. People-watching is a useful activity for any coach, providing a rich resource for insight on how others impact our behaviour. Any type of group work is an opportunity to learn more about how humans operate as social animals, even those individuals with a more introverted preference. Our need for connection is innate – or perhaps partly learnt. The degree to which that ability to socialize and connect becomes a need varies from individual to individual. One thing is for sure: normally functioning human beings need to be with other human beings.

That need for connection is possibly one of the reasons why coaching groups can be deeply rewarding and satisfying. Connecting with others is not without its downsides and can sometimes be both challenging and frustrating. If you've been coaching individuals one-to-one for a while then you'll have reached a steady state of coaching performance. You'll have set patterns of behaviours and know roughly what to expect from the inter-personal dynamic. How does taking the step from one-to-one coaching to group coaching feel? I'm guessing that you might have a feeling of fear somewhere. Perhaps it's a feeling of apprehension or uncertainty about what to expect. One of the most cited fears around group coaching or working with groups of people is how to work with the group dynamic.

A working definition of group dynamic

The group dynamic is the way a group behaves and the socio-psychological processes that underpin the behaviour. Once the group is formed, those behaviours and thinking processes start to create patterns for how the group interacts – both within the group and outside with other groups.

In other words, it is the way people behave when they're with other people and the level of predictability of that behaviour. The group in effect becomes a living entity that is greater than the sum of its individual parts. Studying group dynamics is an important activity for a group coach because it gives you a lens through which to interpret and understand behaviours within the group and between groups. Where there is a strong group dynamic the individual becomes linked with that group and the social identity takes precedence, even to the extent that people are likely to sublimate their individual personality to the personality of the group. We will investigate this aspect of group dynamics later on when exploring some of the key research into how groups behave and why.

Managing and coping with the group dynamic is perhaps one of the key differentiators between group and individual coaching. It requires of the coach a higher degree of observation and interpretative skills around what's happening in the group process. In the previous chapter I discussed an experience on a course where Day 2 always seemed to deliver certain group behaviours. The fact we were able to predict this was certainly about observation and keen awareness of how the group dynamic was playing out. Even if you've been coaching groups for many years, keeping that keen awareness is challenging, particularly when you are juggling a number of other activities in your mind. Sometimes we only become aware of the impact of the group dynamic after the event. This is perhaps one of the reasons why supervision is so crucial – it provides an opportunity to uncover the learning and remember what you've observed and experienced. And sometimes it can be as easy as asking the group: What do we think is happening within the group process at the moment? How might this be playing out in the discussion/topic in hand?

In the previous chapters we took a close look at the group coaching process, but the individuals who perform the tasks within the process ultimately determine what happens. A process of and by itself is not enough. Human beings are perfectly flawed – we are designed to learn through experience and experimentation, so part of that learning process means we won't always get things right first time. Coaches who've studied neurolinguistic programming (NLP) know that what we think and believe impacts massively on how we behave. Each time the group meets, the individuals within it bring their multiple experiences, beliefs, values, assumptions and self-views that impact how they interact with others; this becomes synthesized at a group level and contributes to how the group behaves. Maintaining a child-like curiosity about the group, about me as the coach and what my role is within the group enables a rich learning experience for everyone. It is intriguing how one intervention works really well with one group and yet falls flat with another. What's happening that's made the difference? What do you think? Below are some questions to help you engage your child-like curiosity. Build up your own list of questions and use these as part of your evaluation process after each session.

Exercise

- What experiences have you had with groups?

- When the energy flowed and the group was productive what do you think was happening at a group level that contributed to that?

- When there was resistance and low energy, where was that coming from?

- What did you notice about how the group was interacting?

- What have you noticed about groups that work well together?

- What have you noticed about groups that seem to jar?

- What resources from your previous experiences did/can you draw on?

The hypothesis that group coaching can be used at an organization level to optimize and leverage talent has to be thought through by taking into account the whole system. Group dynamics at an organization-wide level become the culture of the organization. We'll talk later about keeping this start position in mind because group coaching has a potential downside if you are using it in an organization. In effect, you might be creating subcultures through the groups you are coaching – these become individual units. Leveraging talent is about synthesizing these groups so that they are greater than the sum of their parts.

Many years ago in an organization long since defunct, there was a group of coaches who were change agents for a massive transformation programme. The coaches became the 'in group' and everyone else was on the outside. At least, that's how I experienced it. The overriding purpose of the group – to bring about positive change and stimulate creativity – seemed to be lost because of this group dynamic. If you weren't on the inside, you didn't know the right language to use and weren't considered to be where it was at! A cautionary tale if you use group coaching as talent leverage. I'll explore inclusive and exclusive talent strategies later – the lesson is to know what you're getting into before you take the first step.

Let's bring the beginner's mindset right back into focus. It's ok to feel a little fearful about stepping into something different – it's just part of the learning process. And if you've been coaching groups for a long time, maybe you've become so used to group behaviours that perhaps you're operating in an unconscious competence state all the time so that the learning process is not so keen. To work well with any group requires an 'in the moment' awareness of what's happening in the group dynamic. You don't need to be a psychoanalyst but you do need to understand some fundamental principles of how we behave in groups and how our individual behaviours may sometimes become sublimated or change completely when we're with other people. The work of Lewin, Schutz, Tuckman, Cialdini and Zimbardo gives us useful keys to unlock some of the mysteries of group behaviour. Knowing how to make a useful intervention and keep the group alive to the 'click-whirr' nature of social identity is an underlying tool for any group coach. Each of us is subject to our unconscious mind and the default programmes we are set with at birth or learn through the socialization process. Awareness, constant vigilance and proactive thinking are vital attributes for a group coach.

The origin of group dynamics: the term not the reality!

There are many great minds who've contributed to the development of what is now known as 'group dynamics.' The term 'group dynamic' was introduced by Kurt Lewin, who established The Research Centre for Group Dynamics at MIT in 1945. Groups form either on purpose or due to circumstances – something drives them into existence. Lewin's research discovered two core concepts about group process: interdependence of fate and task inter-dependence. The former is where the group identity is born out of a realization that the fate of individuals is linked to the fate of the group. Lewin's heritage perhaps sparked this concept as he cites Jews as an example of this type of group. They are a group interdependent on each other for their fate. The group evolves an identity because of the context. As the coach you may well be coaching individuals who are part of a particular function that is being changed. So each individual identifies with the function – if one falls, we all fall, strength-in-numbers-type reasoning.

It is more likely though that task interdependence is the area that your group will be operating from. This is where the members are dependent on each other and work together to reach their goals. The purpose of coaching a group versus coaching an individual is to leverage the totality of the group to learn and support each other in the learning and self-development process. Individuals become reliant on the group to help them with that process – even though they have individual goals. It's about the whole being more than just the sum of the parts:

> He [Lewin] was able to argue that people may come to a group with very different dispositions, but if they share a common objective, they are likely to act together to achieve it (MK Smith, 2001).

Team coaching and group coaching both share an attribute that helps create a potentially positive group dynamic: a shared objective. The team objective will probably be one overarching objective, whereas the overarching objective in group coaching is learning and personal development, with the specific content of the learning and development down to each individual.

Returning to the exercise above take a look at your answer to the question: When there was resistance and low energy, where was that coming from? I suspect that some answers might relate to the overriding objective of the coaching. One team I worked with were functionally related – in other words, the organization chart suggested they were a team. The reality was very different. The missing ingredient was the shared common objective. Ostensibly they all bought into the shared team goal. How I experienced them as team was very different. I hypothesized that there were many hidden agendas and the team was in fact a collection of smaller sub-groups – each of which definitely did have shared objectives. This was probably why the behaviours of showing support for certain individuals and tasks and showing either active or passive resistance to others played out. It was an interesting experience and a rich resource for learning about what happens when groups are forced-fit to make a team. As a group coach there is one core lesson to come out of this – know who is in the group, where they're from, how their aspirations fit with other members of the group and what underlying agendas might be hiding ready to sabotage the group process.

If interdependence of task is one of the foundation blocks, then mindset is the other. Will Schutz (1958) developed further concepts around group dynamics based on his research with the US navy. That research explored why some groups performed really well and others didn't. His discovery led to the creation of what is now a popular psychometric tool, FIRO-B. He identified three core needs in human beings: to feel included, to have some control and to feel connected with other human beings. These three needs might be wanted and/or expressed. You might experience this as an individual who has a high need for inclusion but it is left unexpressed. Such people may well demonstrate some passive-aggressive behaviour that indicates something is going on at a deeper level.

> ## Exercise
>
> Based on what you've read so far, spend a few minutes reflecting on your experiences of working in groups. Include experiences not just from your working life but also social interactions and maybe groups you're involved in for pleasure. Remember what you saw, heard and felt, and allow your mind to wander. Now write quickly and without judgement what comes to mind. What feelings can you remember about being included, having control and connecting with people in the groups?
>
> Being alive to your own experiences of groups enables you to connect and link those experiences. This might be a useful exercise for your group as well. The path to self-development, like many other journeys, starts with self-awareness and awareness of others.

The next part of the book explores coaching tools for groups, and I would recommend FIRO-B as a potential tool to help with the 'settling in' process at the beginning of the group coaching relationship. Trust is essential if a group is to really make transformational changes, and being honest about your expressed and wanted needs is part of learning how to communicate even more effectively with others. Even where the group coaching veers more to content there is still value in understanding this since it provides a potential vehicle for resolving any issues that might crop up within the group process. Everything is an opportunity for learning if you choose to treat it as such – even conflict.

Schutz also discovered that where groups are compatible there will be higher levels of productivity. Compatibility includes status, technical ability, social standing and education. I guess this is the concept of 'I like people who are like me.' The significance of this for coaching groups builds on the lesson of knowing who is in the group. The first step to creating success, for example, developing talents, starts with understanding what level of interdependence exists, either through compatibility of individuals or compatibility of the objective. So interdependence and mindset create the environment in which the group process evolves, lives and breathes. There is also a pattern of behaviour that seems to flow naturally and was outlined by Bruce Tuckman (1965), which is a useful aid for working with the group process.

Tuckman developed his model of teams from research carried out whilst working in a think tank to study group behaviour in the US navy. His paper, 'Developmental sequence in small groups', paved the way for an enduring model that today is widely used by many different disciplines. This model is

FIGURE 6.1

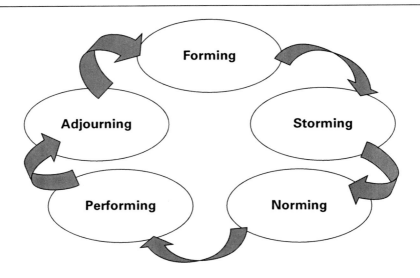

perhaps one of the core models I keep in mind when working with any group. It's my port in a storm when I'm feeling challenged and vulnerable. It's an extremely accessible model and if you've been coaching groups for a while I am sure that this will not be new to you. It also helps to understand how to observe and take notice of behaviour patterns and use these observations to help the group mature. Tuckman's original research paper refers to small groups although now the model mostly refers to teams, but as the research title suggests, the process equally applies to a group. Tuckman's model (Figure 6.1) on team development and behaviour explains an observed process on what high-performing teams do to achieve their outcome: form, storm, norm and perform. Tuckman added 'adjourn' in 1977 based on subsequent research and this stage recognizes that closure is needed to move from performing in one team to forming another team. It is also known as 'mourning' to recognize the 'letting go' process, and some practitioners even call it the celebrating phase. Looking back at your reflections you might spot some of the process stages. The model really clarifies the socialization process around how people work together. The purpose of group coaching is to achieve a goal around shared learning and development, and it's also about understanding how you can work more effectively when you work with other people. So let's have a look at each stage in detail so that when time constraints kick in, you have a way of potentially speeding up the process – potentially.

Forming

When a group of people come together they are a collection of individuals seeking a purpose to collaborate. Forming is an exploratory phase because human beings are designed to generate a threat response when meeting new people for the first time in a group situation (Rock, 2009). During this stage individuals have yet to 'bond' and might have to step outside their comfort zones to create connection. I always observe what happens as people enter the room for the first time and notice who they gravitate towards and their general demeanour. The forming stage is the 'getting to know you' stage. In my experience this is where people test out how much they can trust the others in the group. The group contracting process is fundamental to this stage and may well need revisiting to consolidate this trust. In team terms, this is about getting the right people in the team and making sure they have the right roles, which is crucial if the group is to become a team that achieves its goal. For groups to be effective there also has to be a degree of 'right fit', as explored above. But that's not the only time a team or group forms – when members leave and new members join the team or group, it has to go through the same process of welcoming the new members and showing them how things are done around here – the group norms that have become established over time. There is something at this stage that is about the socialization of the group. For the individual it's about assessing who is in the group and discovering shared interests and starting the process of shared identity. This is also the stage where the end goal or outcome is discussed for the first time as a group. The forming stage, therefore, occurs both when the group comes together for the first time and when something changes.

Storming

This is always the 'interesting' stage in team and group development because it's about the group testing the boundaries, ground rules and their position within the group. This is the teenage years of the group! I suspect that if you're new to group work this is the area that provides the most angst. And it's true – it can be quite scary working with a group at this stage. And it can also be exhilarating when they come through it. Keeping a clear head and reflecting back what might be happening will help develop group awareness and reach a positive outcome. This is the disruptive creativity surfacing within the group along with identity processing. So you might experience competitiveness among team members and sometimes out-and-out conflict. Jockeying for position can also accompany this stage, along with game playing and 'showing off'. All of these behaviours are part of the natural process of a group transitioning through the evolutionary stages. It's important to recognize that this might evoke emotional responses in you as the coach. So just trust the process and help the group work with it, because it can be a healthy and productive stage in the maturation of the group. Teams and groups that go on to achieve great things develop a way of managing this conflict so that it becomes a healthy way of airing differences and getting things out into the open. The trick is to help create a way for the group to discuss, declare, solve, resolve, and move on. Keep your ego out of the process at this stage; don't take it personally and stay focused on coaching the group through this necessary discomfort. Learning is sometimes like the butterfly struggling to escape the cocoon. If it stays in the comfort of the cocoon it will never emerge in all its glory.

Trust is a key success factor in whether or not the team will move on – so something that helps the group create a safe and trustworthy environment is crucial. This is where the contracting process gets tested. In dysfunctional teams and groups, they never move beyond this stage usually because there is insufficient trust and lack of shared goal. Storming is about laying your cards on the table and really getting into the nitty-gritty around the shared learning goal and group support process.

Norming

This is the steady-state functioning of the group. Some teams never reach this stage because they are unable to work through the discomfort stage of normal group development. On the surface the term 'norming' probably sounds straightforward but it's a great place for a group to be. They've worked out how to get along and all know what their identity is within the group; they know what tasks they've got to achieve and have internalized the 'standard operating procedures' of the group. The habits they've developed as a group are serving them well and there is a high degree of trust and collaboration. They are also pretty good at taking action and making progress, and understand how they are accountable to themselves and the group. *But* there is a danger that if a team stays too long at the 'norming' stage complacency will creep in and motivation will wane. At this stage the group can pretty much function without too much hassle and the coach both works collaboratively and can challenge to inspire energy. The group has integrated and reached a stage of balance. Norming is about finding a balance without becoming complacent – it's that challenge that keeps the group moving. The next stage is where the transformation really takes root.

Performing

One of the most satisfying stages in the group's development is the performing stage. The members have moved beyond their comfort zone and are willing to keep stretching the limits to see where it takes them. Behaviours at this stage include an unstinting thirst for learning experiences and a desire to understand what's really happening. This is the stage when the group can leverage the sum of the parts and capitalize on the talents of each individual in a way that delivers much more than if they were working on their own. Collaborations may well emerge beyond the natural boundaries of the group coaching, and the group behaves with openness and members are comfortable with their vulnerability – as a group and as individuals within the group. The work at this stage is continuous improvement and keeping the group challenged and refreshed so that they can continue to get great results. The coach also works with this energy and acquires a sense of freedom in the way they coach the group. In reality this stage takes time, effort and commitment from everyone and I have rarely worked with groups who've wanted to commit to this level of discipline around the group process. That's just my experience – but I know it when I see it! This is the stage at which you truly optimize talents and is where the talent becomes talented! Neuroscience has now reached a level of maturity where we can make statements about how the brain functions with a higher degree of certainty. Doidge (2008) and Shenk (2011) discuss the research that illustrates why this last stage in the group process is the proverbial jewel in the crown. The research has substantiated claims that it takes around 10,000 hours of deliberate practice to master something. The experiments demonstrate that when we are learning something new it has to transfer from the short-term to the long-term memory, and this can only happen through revisiting what we've learnt and allowing 'down time' for the brain to do what it needs to process the new stuff.

> the 'tortoises' who seem slow to pick up a skill, may nevertheless learn it better than their 'hare' friends – the 'quick studies' who won't necessarily hold onto what they have learned without the sustained practice that solidifies the learning (Doidge, 2008).

When starting your group coaching journey, bear in mind that the nature of groups and teams does entail deliberate, purposeful action that must be repeated time and again to get it 'in the muscle'. Your role as the coach is to help create an environment for a positive group dynamic. This is about group coaching mastery not skill acquisition. It takes practice and real discipline to keep it in the conscious mind. I am still practising! The coach's role is to know how to add a bit of frisson into the mix so that they constantly challenge the group with new ideas and different perspectives to bolster motivation and keep the learning and development process alive.

Adjourning

Tuckman reflects that the term was coined after attempts to find a rhyme, and this stage was added later to recognize that teams do not last forever in an age of constant flow and flux. This stage is about recognizing the team's achievements, both what's gone well and what could have gone better, and is part of the letting go process. Without this formal stage of 'saying goodbye' the process of moving on can be difficult for some. Adjourning is a way of 'grieving' for the old team and enabling a new journey with the next team. This is an important part of the process and very often missed in the group coaching process. When you design your own blueprint think about how the team will say 'goodbye' or maybe 'au revoir'! Is there a celebration process for the group or some other way of recognizing the journey and taking with them the best bits of what's come out of the learning with the group?

The research that Tuckman did clearly identified patterns of behaviours and what those behaviours might mean. His model is a useful and thought-provoking tool that has perhaps become a hostage to its own success. The model has crept into the social psyche and most people in the business world will be able to recite the terms form, storm, norm, perform without really examining what that might mean. The next time you are in a situation where a group is setting off on its journey, pay close attention to the group process and really experience what the research is about. As I said at the beginning of this chapter, it's fascinating how we behave in groups. To have an ability to 'step outside' the action so that you as the coach are truly absorbing the dynamics at play is one of the reasons that coaching groups provides a different type of learning compared with one-to-one work. The journey continues with more recent research into group behaviours.

Social psychology in groups

Coaching people in groups can be more challenging than one-to-one because of the processes we inherently operate with – usually without being aware, as demonstrated above. The ability of others to influence our behaviours can create both positive and negative tensions within the group that the coach then has to cope with and either ameliorate or build on. Each of us has a habitual response to social stimuli and part of the coaching process is to bring this in to our awareness so that we can exert choice.

> Again I had a real buzz from working with people by telephone... Because when you work with people by telephone even more so than face to face – and this was referring back to the days when I was selling by telephone – it was a leveller... The fact that working with the telephone was a great leveller has implications for the group because not getting visual clues, actually working with voice only, takes some of the interference out of the dynamic and frees up both coach and coachees to explore what's happening in neutral territory.
>
> Angela Dunbar, master clean language and emergent knowledge coach

Dr Robert Cialdini's (2007) seminal work on influence talks about six factors that influence our behaviour. There are two factors that provide the group coach with help: social proofing and consistency.

Social proofing

Social proofing is our need to copy others who we perceive to be similar to ourselves. On the downside, social proofing can mean that if a group is behaving in an unproductive way, this behaviour will be reinforced by the need to be like others. So, everyone identifies with the behaviour and starts to 'act out' that behaviour. On the plus side, where the group is demonstrating productive behaviours, then provided the individual members perceive themselves to be similar, they will start to replicate those positive behaviours. Your choice of language in coaching the group can help the group to associate with positive social proofing, for example, referencing other groups you've experienced coaching who shared similar experiences/attributes/issues etc, and then directing the group behaviour in a similar way. The underlying message being: 'If you want to have what the other group had, then this is what you can do.' What you are doing here is providing examples of productive behaviours that the group might identify with so that they can copy those behaviours. Clearly you do have to be keenly aware that you are choosing to direct the group and ensure that you act with absolute integrity. The default position should always be first to provide reflective learning experiences and develop the group's observation skills. You might share with the group that they may be subject to this influence factor and ask them what they've noticed.

Consistency

Consistency is the need to do what you say you will do. Research suggests that the brain, or rather the mind, seeks balance and consistency. In other words, when you hold a belief the mind seeks data that supports that belief, and your actions will be consistent with that belief. One of the core benefits of coaching people in groups lies in this influence factor. After all, you want individuals to be committed to actions and be accountable. Essentially this factor is all about accountability – once you have publicly made a commitment you are more likely to carry through. The downside means it can be uncomfortable for coachees coming back to subsequent sessions if they haven't been able to carry out their actions. They might come back to the next session realizing that those actions weren't important enough in view of other priorities in their lives. So that element of public accountability needs to be handled carefully and supportively. Yes, you want people to take action and yes, you want the group to hold them to account. What you don't want is a kangaroo court!

The whole is greater than the sum of its parts

Any discussion about group dynamics and, more importantly the group directive, would not be complete without mentioning Dr Philip Zimbardo, who was the lead researcher in the Stanford Prison Experiment. The experiment was conducted in 1971 at Stanford University in Palo Alto, California. The experiment was designed to investigate the behaviours of prisoners and guards and was planned to last for two weeks. Within the grounds of Stanford university, Zimbardo and his colleagues created a 'prison'. They selected student volunteers for the experiment and randomly assigned them as prisoners or guards. The experiment started with the help of the local police force who arrested the volunteers assigned to 'prisoner' roles at their homes. During the course of the experiment it became apparent that even though the students knew it was an experiment, they adapted and performed their roles so realistically that the experiment had to be stopped before it reached the end of the first week. The level of abuse and degradation suffered by the 'prisoners' and the sadistic behaviour of the 'guards' was quite astonishing. Even more so, because they all knew that it wasn't real – they were merely acting out a role! The Stanford Prison Experiment demonstrates clearly that groups behave in a way that might differ wildly from how the separate individuals would normally behave. These 'situational forces' have a massive influence on the group and can sometimes mean that the group takes on an energy of its own that then directs the behaviours of the group. It is very unlikely that you will ever experience the extreme behaviours encountered in Zimbardo's experiment. However, it is useful to know that sometimes unproductive behaviour could stem from 'situational forces' outside the coaching itself. Being in the moment and awake to what else might be happening for this group of people outside the coaching experience is crucial if you are to help the group learn and move forward. As Zimbardo (2007) notes: 'Too often we function on automatic pilot.'

Here's my take on what Zimbardo tells us and how you can help yourself and the group function well:

- Take yourself off automatic pilot. Stay present and connected to what's happening in the here and now with the group. Keep your radar switched on to what's happening in the wider system at play.

- Maintain personal responsibility for your role within the group – even if it sometimes feels uncomfortable. Leave your ego at home and think about the bigger picture: what's really going on?

- Recognize that the feeling of discomfort might stem from an inherent need to 'fit in' and play your role. Doing what is expected is not always the optimal way to learn.

- Focus on being you, an individual who can exert choices and take accountability.

- Respect others for being themselves regardless of whether or not they are like you.

There is a natural tendency for groups within organizations to take on a life of their own. Being open to how status and hierarchy within the organization might be affecting the way the group is assigning roles and people are acting within those roles is a key part of how coaching groups is different from coaching individuals. The stimulus–response aspect of role assignment is one of the most striking things about the Prison experiment – breaking that pattern and bringing awareness to the system it creates is a crucial part of your role as coach. Here's an example from Lorna McDowell, MD of Xenergie:

Team of five senior managers – there were two senior managers who absolutely hated each other... we ended up almost having to do a therapy session. We had to stop the coaching and take these two individuals out for an hour – I took one and my colleague took the other... And what was interesting... There was a very, very acrimonious dispute between two people... It was so destructive to the rest of the group. The purpose of the coaching was to bring the team, quite a young team, together to get a better sense of their vision and direction and we found that this issue between these two people [was quite destructive]... It was an interesting dynamic because we had this tension between the two mammoth companies and it was all being played out in the relationship between these two people. It was very complex. It wasn't just as simple as a dispute between two people, so there was a systems thing in there, a cultural thing in there, the fact they were all inexperienced... That was very, very challenging and was back early on in some of the senior team coaching that we were doing. So the lessons were that we just had to work intuitively in the moment.

Group processes are a rich resource for learning. They provide an extra tool for the coach to tap into and a means for individuals to learn more about how they connect with other human beings. Developing together is the motto behind group coaching work. One experience I had many years ago feels as fresh now as it did then. At the end of a tiring day working with a group we sat down to do a little reflection of what had happened during the day. The conversation started and then, as if someone had sprinkled magic dust into the room, the energy changed. The group became peaceful and there was palpable trust in the atmosphere. One person started talking – one who had been very quiet during most of the day and who I had suspected had an introvert preference. For them, just the act of talking within the group was a challenge. What came next blew me away. They shared their vulnerability about what it was like for them being in the group and how they were feeling. As they continued talking, tears formed in their eyes and the emotion flowed into the room. Suddenly the group understood at a visceral level what it meant to really trust each other and how they would 'be' as team moving forward. This is what being greater than the sum of the parts means. When the group has a collective moment charged with meaning and insight.

KEY POINTS

- The need for connection with other human beings drives our behaviour and the group coaching dynamic provides a rich resource for observing and learning about how this is manifested.

- It's ok to feel apprehensive about working with groups if you've had little experience of this so far. Stay connected with your own experiences and use what you notice to leverage group learning.

- We are never free from our inherent socialization experiences and instinctive behaviour traits. Coaching people to a level of awareness is part of the group learning process.

- All of the skills and knowledge learnt through being coached with others can be applied to life experiences outside the coaching frame. Coachees have the potential to learn how to adopt and adapt social skills through the group experience. They awake from the automatic responses they have learned or intuited.

- Trust, interdependence, sharing vulnerability and willingness to challenge how the group interacts are some of the facets that deliver meaningful group coaching experiences.

PART THREE
Tools and processes

Contracting for 'success'

The foundation for success starts with 'contracting' in the broadest sense of the word. This is not about the written contract, it's about the socio-psychological contract and this means declaring, understanding and 'dealing with' everyone's needs, wants and expectations for the coaching journey on which you are about to embark, and this includes your own needs, wants and expectations as the coach. We often don't have an awareness of the 'contracts' we create in our daily lives and the tacit assumptions we all have about social norms – that 'everyone knows how to behave' or 'they know what I want' and generally how we'll interact with each other. This is usually the starting point for disagreements and disenchantment – because these assumptions are not declared and this sows the seeds for potential difficulties. In coaching terms, disappointments and a sense of failure often occur when we set un-realistic expectations or don't articulate what's really going on for us as at a deeper level. We create a set of assumptions against which we measure our-selves and others, which means that our journey to the promised land of 'success' is not founded on solid rock. How you evaluate success and the results you and your group obtain is fundamentally reliant on having a strong contracting process and demonstrating congruence. Contracting therefore is the start of the measurement process, since this creates the context in which you and your coachees will experience working together.

The contract

Even though the coaching contract isn't a legal contract it does have some similar characteristics to draw on to make the metaphor work:

- Each party is free to enter into the contract.
- The contract has to be specific and meaningful to each party – the terms have to be clear.

- All parties have to 'give' something for the contract to work – the notion of 'consideration'.

- There is an agreement based on the above.

Keeping this simple check list in the back of your mind when starting to work with your group will help you establish clear contracts on which to develop your coaching relationship. The principles behind this are:

- All coachees can choose whether or not they wished to be coached, and coaches can choose who they work with and what areas they coach in.

- The ground rules, scope and boundaries of your coaching relationship are clearly spelled out in unequivocal terms.

- Both you and the coachees commit to give something in return for the coaching, whether this is time, energy, action or anything else that is relevant for the coaching relationship. It's a two-way flow of time, energy, resources and commitment between the coach and coachee.

- Everyone knows what they're signing up for and agree to the specific terms.

The final point is that, like any other form of contract, if one party 'breaches' the terms it should be clear what the consequences will be. In relation to ground rules, this might manifest in the sanctions that you or the group apply to anyone who transgresses the ground rules. And this is why it's important to be absolutely crystal clear what the ground rules are. The notion of 'natural justice' has to be present for groups to feel that a 'safe' environment is created for them to be coached.

How contracting is different for group coaching

Before exploring how contracting is different for group coaching than for one-to-one coaching, spend a few minutes thinking about what might make that true. What factors come into play within group coaching that aren't present in one-to-one coaching relationships? Let's imagine that you have in your hands a Rubik's cube – the toy that gained popularity back in the 1980s. Your task is to line up all the different colours along the three dimensions of the cube. And therein lies the challenge of contracting in the group environment – particularly when the groups are in organizations and where all of the individuals have different managers. There might be one overall sponsor for the activity but their role will be to act as a conduit for all of those needs, wants and expectations from the different parties. And that's before you've taken account of the individual coachees' needs, wants and expectations. At Figure 7.1 there is a simple representation of what this might look like. As we move through the levels of complexity (Figure 7.2) to the network of people involved in having a say about the coaching (Figure 7.3), we can see that the coach's job of aligning the different expectations from the coaching will be challenging to say the least.

FIGURE 7.1

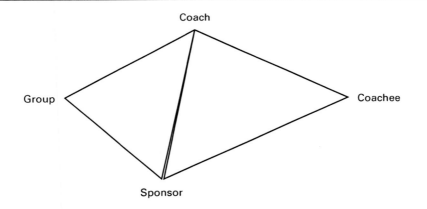

FIGURE 7.2

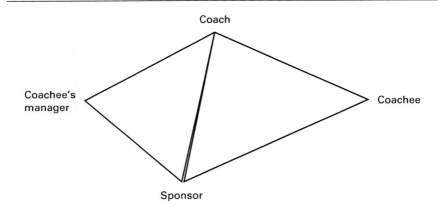

FIGURE 7.3

Manager

Coachee   Coachee

Manager   Manager

Coach   Coachee

In the previous chapters I outlined some of the areas you will need to consider in developing your group coaching process, and contracting is one of those areas. How will you, for example, ensure that the sponsor has accurately reflected the needs and expectations of the management community they represent? Instinctively I would want everyone in the room at the same time to explore these types of questions. Practically, this is usually difficult to achieve because of the demands on time of the people within organizations and the problem of coordinating availability. Inevitably someone will be unable to make the session. One way I've countered this problem is by having brief telephone meetings with all stakeholders to explore with them what they're expecting and what they know about the process. As is the nature with groups though, one-to-one they may tell you things that in a wider group become moderated by the group or are not even mentioned.

As a group coach working in an organizational setting, your task in the contracting process is not only to coach the group but to 'coach' the people who have links with the group, either directly or indirectly via the sponsor, to ensure that you are creating a holistic contract. We will explore systems later on in the book; at this stage let's just acknowledge that the contract is part of the system in which you are working with the group. The level of complexity increases as you move from coaching individual clients who seek group coaching through to organizations using group coaching across their business. Group coaching contracts are about achieving balance and fairness for all, including the coach. And this is where boundary management starts to become even more important. Creating a group coaching contract shares similar characteristics with consultancy contracts and requires a lot more planning and coordination than in a simple one-to-one coaching relationship.

Why contracting is important

Many years ago when I trained to be a facilitator, long before coaching became popular, one of the first mantras I learnt was: 'Time spent in preparation is never wasted; and time spent discussing, refining and agreeing the contract and ground rules is part of that preparation.'

On a practical level this means that the more time you spend up front working with your clients *before* the coaching sessions start and getting crystal clear about what you'll be doing, how you'll be doing it and who is responsible for what, the greater the pay-off later when you get into the work of coaching the group. You should allow enough time in your process to do a thorough job with the contracting phase, as this is the stage at which potential future issues may arise – or at the least indicators of the areas in which you are most likely to be challenged in your coaching. Often as coaches we like to keep things positive and for some coaches the contracting phase can be uncomfortable; in a group coaching context, this is the time to really clarify what you're there to do as the coach, have open conversations about the scope of the coaching and how you will work with the coachees, identify what is likely to work and what isn't, and establish their commitment to the coaching process. Robust conversations are sometimes required to really get under the skin of what is expected and wanted – this is the stage of the coaching process where you use both your coaching skills and your consultancy skills. You want to know up front what the foundations are upon which you are all going to build the coaching relationship. The contracting conversations are a means of declaring both the practical and the intangible. For example: how you will work with confidential issues; what you will do as the coach when you spot something that might suggest a systems-type challenge rather than a coaching challenge; what you will do if coachees miss sessions; timings of sessions and so on. Even if you aren't able to have the full session mentioned above with all the stakeholders in an organizational setting, it is worth having separate pre-meetings with the 'sponsor' and each of the coachees in addition to a three-way meeting with the 'sponsor', coachees and coach before the coaching sessions start, to ensure everyone has a clear understanding and agreement about what will happen with the group coaching. A post-coaching three-way meeting with the sponsor, group and coach to review the coaching after the sessions are complete is also a way of moving into the adjournment stage that Tuckman describes in his model. There is closure on the work that has been done and an opportunity to open up discussions about what happens so as to prepare for the next steps.

Contracting, therefore, occurs before, during and after the coaching sessions, and in NLP terms you might wish to think of this as pre-frame, re-frame and de-frame! The pre-framing of 'success' is about understanding what's going on that will support or deter the progress of the group and the individual coachees. It's also important to understand the level of 'interference' that might seep in from the system in which the coachees 'live'. Success starts with expectations, no matter how the coachees, and if relevant the organization, define 'success'. The initial contracting phase is about coachees, and the organization if relevant, selecting the coach and the coach agreeing to the assignment, having established there is a basic platform on which to coach (coachability assessment). During this phase the process of declaring expectations and naming them is crucial. One model used in relationship coaching suggests that after the attraction phase there will be tacit assumptions that turn into expectations about the relationship. If these expectations don't get met, each time they are transgressed grievances will start to accumulate. Over time these grievances develop into bigger and bigger problems until eventually the relationship breaks down. The underlying factor is that none of the expectations or grievances are aired, so neither party understands what it is they have done, or not done, to cause the dispute. It is much better to declare expectations up front, even if is sometimes uncomfortable. For example, the matter of payment and payment terms for coaching services can be an uncomfortable topic for some coaches (and clients); addressing them up front means there will be less chance for disputes and avoids a situation in the future where you feel aggrieved because you haven't been paid on time, or the client feels aggrieved because they don't understand how you're charging for your services. Addressing in real time any potential issues around the 'contract' that you, the group and, where relevant, the sponsor have agreed means things can be resolved immediately rather than left to bubble under the surface. Contracting is a continuous process and it is no surprise that boundary management and contracting are the two key areas that crop up most in conversations with other coaches – probably because they're the conduit for expectations that help create a safe environment for coachees and support the coach in keeping that space sacred. Your core objective as a coach is to help create a transparent, collaborative and supportive relationship with your client and coachees so that you can together achieve your own version of 'success'.

Qualification process

There are two aspects to the pre-coaching stage of the contracting: decision making and coachability. These help you qualify coachees and clients in or out of your process. You always have a choice about the groups you coach, even if there are consequences attached to those choices.

Decision making

There are three areas I cover with coachees and clients to help them make a decision about whether or not group coaching is right for them, and this is a two-way process. In other words, if I feel that group coaching is not the right approach I will say so. Similarly, if I have misgivings that the individual is not really committed to the coaching process I will also declare that at this stage. We often forget that we have a choice too about who we coach and which method we use. Our clients and coachees pay us for the exercise of our intelligence – if we have a sense that coaching isn't going to help then we should declare that, in the spirit of openness and in the service of our clients and coachees. I have a preference for grouping things in threes, so my decision-making process has three elements:

- Whether the group coaching is going to be helpful and is the right approach for the presenting topic; for example, there might be other interventions that are more useful or helpful rather than group coaching.
- How comfortable they feel about me as their coach.
- Whether they're really committed to taking action and changing their behaviour.

Coachability

This second aspect of the pre-coaching stage centres on the individual coachee's 'coachability' score. How open are they to the coaching process. Again, I use three indices to help with this, and talk these through with my coachees in an open and up-front way so that neither of us in any doubt as to what the coaching process involves, and I involve the sponsor client in these discussions where I work in an organization. I didn't follow this approach in a systematic way when I first started my coaching practice; it is only with experience that I've come to realize the value of this stage in the pre-contracting phase.

- Have you had coaching before but it hasn't 'worked'?
- How would you assess your level of personal commitment on a scale of 1–10 to turn up on time and complete assignments?
- Do you know specifically and in what way you want to change/improve?

Of course, it is impossible for the coachees to know exactly at this stage what is likely to come up in the coaching and how they are likely to cope with the level of commitment required. What it does is set an expectation that they will be required to put in effort and it's not just a matter of the coach doing all the work. What it also demonstrates is that you will be prepared to have challenging conversations that are designed to move the coachees out of their comfort zones and into their talent zones – and that's what the coaching process helps them do.

Contracting out at the end of the group coaching assignment

Elegant endings flow naturally from the pre-framing of the relationship. In effect, you set the ground work up front for how you will disengage from the coaching assignment at the end. Sometimes the coaching assignment will end before the scheduled programme of sessions – for example, if organizational changes occur or the group of coachees decides to stop the process. Give consideration to this in the way you pre-frame your contract with all the stakeholders and coachees. One thing you could consider is whether a post-assignment review after 6 months would be helpful for the client and coachees. You might also consider asking for formal feedback by way of a questionnaire. And of course there is the post-coaching review meeting mentioned earlier, which is a similar format to the pre-coaching meeting – this time the focus is on restating the original aims and objectives for the coaching and checking back where everyone is 'now' in relation to these. The contracting out phase serves as a reminder of the 'reason why' the client and coachees started their learning development process. It also provides data to help you, as the coach, decide what you will take forward to other group coaching assignments and what you will let go. It becomes part of your continuous professional development process. Focusing on ending the coaching assignment elegantly is as important as creating a positive frame up front. Holding the space for the client and coachees is part of how you contract before, during and after the assignment. Elegant endings provide the means to consolidate learning, give the psychological 'full stop' and plan your next steps to maintain momentum.

The 'ground rules' in group coaching

Contracting at its simplest level establishes the norms that you will adhere to in working together – that is, the expected behaviours you will operate. Let's return to the concept of socio-psychological norms. The 'socio' part relates to how we interact with others – the social aspect of being human. The 'psychological' part relates to how we think, and feel, about how we are with others. And herein lies the rub of contracting: we are seeking to discover what people find acceptable in the way they interact with others and to disclose how they might be feeling about that interaction. In group coaching terms this is perhaps a new skill for the coach who hitherto has worked on a one-to-one basis. Working with a collection of individuals and asking them to declare what's going on for them 'beneath the surface' requires skilful handling, keen listening and rapport building. It is an opportunity for you as the coach to model these skills for the coachees and can provide a learning opportunity in advance of the coaching you are about to initiate. Contracting and the contracting process are great tools for your coachees to learn, and when I train others in coaching I use this as both the contracting session and the first input session of the day – a parallel-learning opportunity.

There is also the explicit and implicit nature of the contract: what is formalized in the contracting process and what emerges and becomes established through regular interaction. The declared ground rules are the expressed or explicit contract that the group forms. They will start to develop other emergent norms as they become more familiar with each other and relax into the group setting. If you remember back to the chapter where we looked at the Tuckman model of groups, then the implicit norms of the group will start to emerge as they reach the storm and, hopefully, perform stages. For the coach, it is helpful to facilitate discussions with the group about what they are noticing about how the group is working. Here are some sample questions to get you started. Your observations will direct your own questions and the questions below fall naturally from my unconscious mind based on my experiences of working with groups. Yours will be different.

- What have they noticed about some of the things they raised at the first session around how the group will work and where they are now?

- What has happened with regard to their expectations about how they might work together?

- What are they pleased about in relation to how the group is working?

- Are there any areas that might not have lived up to expectations?

- What have they been doing that's contributed positively to the group?

- What have they been doing that's detracted from the group?

- Were they aware of it at the time, or on reflection?

- How do they experience the energy in the group?

The questions are designed to uncover the implicit ground rules that the group have adopted and, in bringing them to their awareness, allow the group to decide whether these rules are helpful or not. This is a useful exercise to do part-way through the coaching process as a means of re-contracting with the group and checking where they're at in relation to their own measures of success. Every intervention you use as the coach is an opportunity for learning – provided you do this consciously and positively. The aim is always around learning and being curious; therefore pre-framing this type of session in this way helps our naturally critical tendencies to stay away!

Exposing potential points of difference or conflict at this stage helps to manage expectations about what is and isn't possible from the coaching process. The ecology questions found in NLP, such as 'How fair is this to all concerned?' 'How does it serve you?' 'How does this fit with your life, home, other goals?' are helpful here in checking for congruence. If there is no real worth in participating in group coaching, this is the stage at which the coachee can choose whether or not to continue. There is always a choice and if individuals discover through the contracting phase there isn't enough benefit and worth to them in proceeding, they have always the right to exit from the process. Contracting is a mutual activity and no one party has more sway than another. Coaching has to be entered into freely, otherwise the individual will never truly engage in the process and the learning process itself will falter through lack of commitment.

Below I offer a suggested framework for working through that first session. It is intended to be a loose framework to help collect your thoughts and trigger ideas about questions and topics to cover. The aim of that first session is to get things out onto the table so that they can be discussed, reviewed, discarded or agreed upon. How you do it depends on the group. I have suggested one contracting tool in the Tools part of this book. I would encourage you to be as creative as possible and keep in mind that your role is to create a safe space and hold the space so that the coachees feel comfortable to explore how they want to work together. And also how they want you to work with them, and what you want from them to ensure you release your best possible coaching skills and talents.

Initial group coaching session and creating collaborative relationships

Aims of the session:

- Find out if any questions have arisen since we last spoke – what has come up for you since we last met?
- To clarify the role of the coach – what do you need, want and expect and what do they need, want and expect from you?
- To reassure client about confidentiality – and be honest about what is possible in relation to confidentiality. What realistically is likely to happen with information that the coachees bring to the session? What do they want, need and expect and what will they do in return for this?
- To find out how the coachees want to be coached – what degree of challenge, support, encouragement, input. How you will review this during the process of the coaching. Joint responsibility for coaching. How much do you want to transfer your skills to the group so that they become self-managed?
- To find out what the coachees would like the coach to do if they get stuck – how will they know and how will you know that they're stuck? What are the options?
- To explain that for the client to get the best value from the coaching you may need to interrupt them from time to time, or stop them to get them back on track – what might the ground rule be around this?
- Value of feedback – from you as the coach during the sessions, from the coachees during and after each session, and formally at pre-agreed intervals depending on how long the group coaching process lasts. Timely feedback means timely action – afterwards is possibly too late!

Closure and contracting

It seems appropriate to end this chapter by recapping thoughts on closure as part of contracting. The post-coaching-assignment contracting discussion is about discussing the thoughts, feelings and outcomes that the coachees and sponsor have about the coaching process. It is at this stage that thoughts return to what was expected of results likely to be obtained. Sometimes, the results are different from those expected – which is either a positive or a negative depending on the results obtained. It is useful to review what led to those results, what might be done differently and how each role in the process contributed to those results. In organizational settings this is the time at which to bring into the discussions the topic of the system in which the coachee 'lives'. It is important to work with the coachees to find the learning opportunities rather than focusing purely on the results. After all, the results happened because of actions that were taken either by the coachees or by other 'players' in the system. Working with the coachees through this complex maze hopefully will help elucidate further opportunities for growth and development. Asking for feedback on the process is a useful activity to highlight opportunities for the coach to learn what might be done differently next time. As we've established, the contract-closure discussion is the reverse of the pre-contracting process – yes, you want to get all the learning out on the table, but the purpose is for review, learning and reflection now that the activities have taken place. The ground rules around honesty and openness that you hopefully outlined in the pre-contracting phase are applied to pull out how well the process worked for your coachees, their sponsor where relevant and you.

'Success' starts with judgement-free understanding of what you expected to do, be or have as a result of the coaching. The contracting process creates the environment in which all parties can experience a judgement-free understanding of what has happened and measure their success in the context of their own reality.

KEY POINTS

- The foundation for great experiences in group coaching starts with the contracting phase.

- Coaching contracts in group coaching are more complex and require a lot more planning and coordination than one-to-one coaching contracts.

- Contracting is a vital step in establishing the basis of the relationship, acknowledging complexities and highlighting potential challenges.

- Ground rules are vital to create group norms of behaviour and help the group moderate its own behaviour so that time can be spent on coaching versus group management.

- Closure is an important part of the contracting phase and cements the learning process.

08 Discovering the right tools

Coaching is a collaborative activity; the coach is not an expert who 'does' things for their clients. They are the guides and facilitators of self-awareness, learning and personal development. Timing is everything, and this is so true when you introduce coaching tools into the group. The most important thing to remember when using any coaching tool or model: the coachees expect you to have expertise and 'know-how' in coaching tools and models; they are also relying on you exercising *judgement* about when to use those tools and models. Sometimes coaches can become a bit too emotionally attached to one model or tool and perceive it as the only tool in their toolkit. In a previous chapter I posed a question: why is it that some groups respond well to a tool whereas the same tool falls flat with another group? There are two factors that help understand this: timing and readiness. So the first lesson about tools is that your ability to exercise sound judgement is your main tool.

Discovery is an interactive process and with practice you can collaborate with groups in a way that allows the essence of the tool to work its magic without the tool taking over. As any coach will have experienced, working with coaching tools is as much an art as it is a technique. In this chapter I'll explore some experiences of introducing tools into the group, and outline a number of tools that seem to work well with groups and also the process you'll follow – remembering of course that the group dynamics will affect the way the tools work for your group. To help you discover group coaching tools the emphasis is on practical tools you can use and experience. There are options in how you use them and potential upsides and downsides that might not be apparent in the black and white print of these pages. The best way to discover cool stuff is through use! Take these blueprints and use, adapt, change, remodel and experiment with them in your groups. Make them your own and use them to discover others.

Please may I use this tool?

Are you willing to experiment? Are you willing to work with me in this way? Seeking permission from the group to use certain coaching tools is a useful exercise – this can be done up front in the contracting process and when introducing the tool into the session. The underlying purpose is to find out how willing the group is to trust you to know which tool to use and be prepared to experiment with different ways of doing and being. Here are some tools to help with the contracting process that might help.

The overall contracting process

Tool name: contracting tool

Tool's purpose

Freedom to explore and develop awareness starts with feeling 'safe' or 'safe enough' to allow for the possibility of growth. The contracting process sets the scene for the space you will help co-create with the group to encourage that freedom.

When do I use it?

It is likely that you have spoken with coachees individually about the way you'll work with them and the group. This tool works well at the first session to build on those individual conversations and start the journey of working together as a group. You might also choose to use some of the questions at the beginning of each session to get everyone both physically and mentally in the room.

What is the process?

You have at least three choices in how you work the process:

- You could start with individual reflection time and then move into group work, or vice versa.
- If you have an even number in the group you could also ask them to work in pairs, taking it in turn to 'interview' each other using the questions and then sharing in the larger group. If you decide to go with this option, another variant could be for the 'interviewer' to relay information about the interviewee back to the group.
- And you could also ask them to form two groups and then share their discussion points in the combined group.

Ask yourself these questions:

> Based on what I've learnt already about these individuals, what are their personalities like? Would they respond to a more reflective space or a space in which they can externalize their thinking? Are there likely to be any personality challenges that could make it uncomfortable for certain individuals to share their thoughts and feelings straight off with the group?

Let's go through each option in turn:

Option 1

1 Before the coachees come into the session, ask them to bring with them any materials you've discussed already. For example, if you've created the coaching brief and contract ask them to bring that along with them.

2 Lay out the room for reflective thinking. Look at the room size, shape, layout, light sources. How could you set the room up so that it's conducive to reflection? Do you want coachees to sit on the floor? Do you want to invite them to get comfortable in their own space? Put yourself in the shoes of your coachees and imagine what it will be like for them walking through the door for the first time. What ambience do you want to create?

3 Greet them as they come into the space and ask them to find somewhere they'll feel comfortable.

4 Before you start the session, ask them to wander round the room and introduce themselves to each other. Help the process by introducing them to one person so that they feel welcomed. How you do this will be determined by your own personal style. Maybe check if they know anyone in the group already.

5 When everyone has arrived start the session by welcoming them and explain what you'll be doing. I'm not going to prescribe how you do this because you will know what feels right for this group of people based on your knowledge of them already. This process step is about getting them comfortable physically and mentally so that they're ready to have their first experience of being together.

6 Ask them to find a space in which they feel comfortable and relaxed; they might wish to sit on the floor or sit at a table. Whatever will help ensure they are ready to reflect.

7 Invite them to consider these questions – What am I holding in mind as I start the group coaching? What do I need to make this a safe space in which to work? What do I bring to this group as a resource?

What is important for other people to know about me? What is important for me to know about other people? How do I expect people in this group to behave? How can you expect me to behave? How will people know when I am feeling comfortable? How will people know when I am feeling uncomfortable? These questions are intended to provide a door to open the way to how we'll work together. There might be other questions that are more meaningful for them. The purpose of the questions is to catalyse discussion later. They might wish to draw symbols or pictures – whatever will bring to life things from within. Make sure they have pens, paper, Post-its etc. Anything that will help them create an external representation of what they might be holding on to.

8 Give them at least 10 minutes to explore the questions. Tell them up front you'll give then an initial 10 minutes and will check in to see where they're at after that.

9 After 10 minutes check to see how they're doing. Do they need longer? Have they had enough time to have sufficient data/answers/information [choose a word that fits the group] to create meaningful discussion. If so, go to the next stage. If not, agree how much longer they need.

Option 2

This option only works where you have an even number in the group. The process is as for Steps 1–5 above.

6 Ask them to find a partner to work with and a space in which they both feel comfortable and relaxed. They might wish to sit on the floor or sit at a table – whatever will help ensure they are ready to reflect.

7 Invite them to consider the questions – What am I holding in mind as I start the group coaching? What do I need to make this a safe space in which to work? What do I bring to this group as a resource? What is important for other people to know about me? What is important for me to know about other people? How do I expect people in this group to behave? How can you expect me to behave? How will people know when I am feeling comfortable? How will people know when I am feeling uncomfortable? These questions are intended to provide a door to open the way to how we'll work together. There might be other questions that are more meaningful for them. The purpose of the questions is to catalyse discussion later. They might wish to draw symbols or pictures – whatever will bring to life things from within. Make sure they have pens, paper, Post-its etc. Anything

that will help them create an external representation of what they might be holding on to.

8 Give them at least 10 minutes to explore the questions. Tell them up front you'll give then an initial 10 minutes and will check in to see where they're at after that.

9 After 10 minutes check to see how they're doing. Do they need longer? Have they had enough time to have sufficient data/answers/information [choose a word that fits the group] to create meaningful discussion. If so, go to the next stage. If not agree how much longer they need.

Option 3

Follow Steps 1–5. Ask them to form two groups and discuss the questions at Step 7 in Option 1.

Tool name: Pandora's box

Tool's purpose

If you focus on what you don't want or on negative thoughts, that's what you get. You will need a beautiful box to use for this tool – one that might be similar to Pandora's!

When do I use it?

This is a particularly useful tool for getting all the negative energy out into the open from the minds of the coachees without it interfering too much with the energy in the room. No one else in the room needs know what negative thoughts the coachees might be bringing to the session, but getting these thoughts out of the coachees' minds means that there is space to open up thinking free from interference. This is probably a good tool to use when you know the coachees or after you have gone through a more detailed contracting process. It's a 'quick start' to getting everyone mentally as well as physically in the room. The trick to this tool is to use almost hypnotic language, pitch and tone, because you want the coachees to tap into their deeper 'unaware' conscious mind, bypassing the conscious mind. It's the stuff that they're carrying with them into the room that might get dropped and cause a mental 'trip hazard' later in the session.

What is the process?

1 Tell the story of Pandora's box – this is a Greek myth from ancient times and among other things tells the story of how Pandora lets

loose all the evils of the world except hopelessness. Here's my version of it. You will be able to find others online and in books on Greek myths. Use poetic licence – the key to the story is the ending!

Zeus, the king of the gods, was furious with Prometheus who had stolen the gift of fire from the gods and given it to humans. Zeus hatches an evil plan to wreak revenge and creates the beautiful Pandora, adding to her allure by giving her a wonderful jewel-encrusted box, sparkling and dazzling. He tells her not to open it. The mighty Zeus then offers the beautiful Pandora to Prometheus as his wife. Wily Prometheus suspects that this is part of Zeus's plan to mete out revenge on him for stealing fire, so refuses to marry her. This doesn't work out so well for him as Zeus chains him to a rock and sends birds of prey to rip out his intestines. His brother Epimetheus, thinking that marrying Pandora is a better choice, accepts her as his wife. The desire to find out what's in the box grows stronger each day and Pandora overcomes her fear of Zeus and, no longer in control of her desire, opens the dazzling curiosity. In an instant all the evils of the world flood out, taking Pandora's breath away. She just manages to shut the box to keep in the last evil – hopelessness. And so, hope remains alive and vibrant in the world.

2 Ask your coachees to take a piece of paper and, quickly and without processing, write down anything that might get in the way of today being a fantastic day for them personally. Work up a script along the lines of: 'Imagine the negative thought passing through your body as it leaves you mind and races down your arm through your pen onto the paper.'

3 Invite them when they have finished writing to remain quiet and place their negative thoughts in Pandora's box.

4 Explain to the group that these negative thoughts will be kept locked away for the rest of the day and will be destroyed later so they will never see them again. They will be free from them. The only thing that will always remain in the box is hopelessness because its sister *hope* is always with us.

5 Summarize this experience by explaining that this story, or metaphor, illustrates how we will work together today. We will keep hope in the mix and lock up any negativity in this box.

Goals and outcomes

Tool name: goal visualization

Tool's purpose

This tool is adapted from one of the *50 Top Tools for Coaching* (Jones and Gorell, 2012) and is designed to tap into the 'other than conscious' or 'out of awareness' part of the mind. It is a guided meditation, although be aware that when working with a group in a business setting the word 'meditation' can have negative connotations or even put people off; therefore, it's up to you whether you describe it as such.

When do I use it?

Ideally this will be at the first session to kick-start the goal or outcome-setting process. I would recommend doing this after you have contracted and checked in with the group to gauge their level of receptiveness. What you say to set this tool up will depend on the energy in the room. Sometimes coachees need space to collect their thoughts before being able to articulate what it is they really want. This type of exercise engages with a different type of being and insight that will probably be different from what they're familiar with. It serves the purpose of interrupting their normal patterns of thinking and seeing so that they are able to intuit their goal and outcome.

What is the process?

1 Help the group relax physically into their space. Check if anyone has any ailments that might hinder this part of the process as you'll be doing some gentle physical relaxation exercises. Ask them to listen to their bodies, and if anything feels uncomfortable choose to stop doing it. They are responsible for just doing enough to help them relax.

2 Ask the group to stand up, feet hip-width apart, and imagine a golden thread running up from the floor all the way up their back and neck and flowing out through the back of their head. This golden thread will keep them connected to the floor and ceiling so that their neck is free, so their head can move forward and up and their back can lengthen and widen. Ask them gently to shake out all their limbs, start with their feet, their legs, one by one, then their arms. Then gently roll their shoulders forwards and back and hunch their shoulders up to their ears and then let go. They can repeat this as many times as they feel comfortable. Listening to their body all the

time and doing just enough to help them relax and release away the tensions of the day. Finally gently and slowly move the head from side to side.

3 When they are ready ask them to breathe in through their mouth on the count of seven and hold for one then breathe out to seven. Repeat this a few times watching all the time to make sure everyone is OK. Make people aware that they can start breathing normally when they are ready. The idea is to fill the abdomen with air and notice the difference between shallow and deep breathing. Remind them to take care of how they feel, and breathe normally when they are ready.

4 When you notice that everyone is ready ask them to find a comfortable position, sitting, standing or lying down. They should be relaxed enough but not on the verge of sleeping!

5 Begin the guided visualization, using your own breathing to help with phrasing and pauses. Below is an adapted script from *50 Top Tools for Coaching*. Adapt this script to suit your audience and on the basis of your own experiences:

'Close your eyes, relax and breathe deeply and slowly.

Notice how your breathing sounds. Notice the breath as it flows in through your nose and flows into your belly. Feel your belly go out and in with the natural ebb and flow of your breath. And as you breathe in, breathe in the colour of positivity and breathe out the colour of negativity.

(Allow at least three breaths.)

On each breath notice how relaxing it is and how the muscles around your eyes relax. (Pause) (As you are watching them be aware of how they start to relax, and continue with the script.)

Now that you are relaxed and comfortable, allow your mind to take you to a place where you would like your life to be, your desired state.

Imagining you are there. Now. And today is a typical morning, and as you get out of bed, notice what is happening around you. What are you seeing? What can you hear? What do you notice in your body – what feelings do you have? What do you want it to be like when you get up on a typical morning?

Remembering how long it has taken you to achieve that goal, that desired state – was it three months, six months, a year, two years? Remember how long it was.

(Pause)

Whatever the timescale, now you're there, waking up on a typical morning having achieved your goal. What can you see, hear and feel that lets you know that you have achieved it now? What is your evidence? Step into that reality and notice the brightness, the shadows, the depths of the colours in your image, the size of the image; what is in the background, middle ground and foreground?

Develop a picture in your mind so that you can touch, hear, smell, see, feel what you are now seeing.

(Pause)

Now add the sounds. What will you hear? Voices, other sounds? What is the volume, pitch, pace, rhythm of those sounds?

What direction do they come from?

Can you hear your own internal dialogue? What are you saying to yourself?

What tone of voice are you using to talk to yourself, excited, congratulatory, or are you in awe of yourself for having achieved your goal?

(Pause)

What does it feel like there as that future you – now?

How do you stand, sit, enter a room, smile?

What does it feel like in your stomach, chest, muscles?

How do you hold your head? How do you talk?

What is your life like now?

(Pause)

Get a very clear idea, using as many senses as you can, of what your life is like now... that you have achieved this change.

(Pause)

Now fast-forward yourself again – a further six months into your future.

You have now been living your dream for a further six months. What is that like?

What is it like to look back to six months ago and realize that you achieved your goal back then?

As you look all the way back to today, what do any obstacles, ones you might have perceived when you came in here today, look like from that vantage point out there in the future?

When you open your eyes, now, you will feel totally refreshed and ready to live that goal!

6 Wait for everyone to open their eyes and mentally come back into the room. Ask them to spend a few minutes in silence, drawing, writing or just pondering on what they've experienced.

7 Choose whether to have a few minutes break after this before going into the group goal setting/outcome process.

Tool name: reframing problems

Tool's purpose

This is an alternative approach to bringing the group mentally into the room and helping them with the goal/outcome-setting process. It's quicker than the visualization process and is based on how our physiology links with our psychology, which can affect our ability to create meaningful and positive goals. Setting this up is very simple and I've used it many times with groups to illustrate the power of mind over matter.

When do I use it?

I use this before working on goals and outcomes and have adapted the process from that described in *50 Top Tools*. It gives the group an experience of how what they're thinking and the way in which they're thinking will affect their ability to create goals that are powerful. It's also a useful entrée into a discussion on the 'towards/away from' goal continuum. Some coachees will have preferences at the extreme ends of this continuum so it's a great way of helping them tap into what that might be about.

What is the process?

1 Ask them to sit or stand comfortably and listen to what you are about to say. Allow the responses to flow naturally through, and experience what happens. Explain that you're not expecting them to give you answers; you are only interested in what happens internally for them.

2 Read out the problem-frame questions in Figure 8.1 below first.

3 Ask them what they experienced as you read out the questions – you don't want their answers to the questions; you want to know what effect the questions had on them.

4 Next read out the outcome-frame questions from Figure 8.1 and repeat Step 3 above.

5 Ask them what they noticed about their responses to the different types of questions.

FIGURE 8.1

Problem Frame	Outcome Frame
Define the problem/issue?	What outcome do you want?
How long has this problem been a problem?	How will you know when you've achieved the outcome?
What is the worst thing about this problem?	What potential solutions can you think of?
How often does it occur?	In order to achieve the outcome, what resources do you need?
Who is to blame?	What resources do you have that will aid the outcome?
Why have you not yet solved this problem?	How can you obtain any additional resources you require?
What are the major hurdles/obstacles of this problem?	Where have you succeeded before, which has been similar to this?
How does it make you feel, see, hear or think?	What steps are required to be taken next?

It is likely that the problem-frame questions will elicit experiences of allotting blame, anger, frustration and so on, whereas the outcome-frame questions will elicit feelings of power, positivity, ideas and so on. Each time it is fascinating to hear what they experienced. It's a very simple and fast way of accessing how we process information and which part of the mind kicks in. This then leads into a discussion about how they will create outcomes and goals for the coaching, and which type of questions they wish to use to help them with this.

Relating to others

Tool name: listening chairs

Tool's purpose

This is one of my favourite group tools because the power is in its simplicity. Coachees learn the different levels of listening and how visual cues can both interfere with and enhance your ability to listen depending on what's happening with the voice inside your head. Drawing out the learning is limited only by your ability to ask follow-on questions and the group's willingness to explore deeper.

When do I use it?

You can use it at any stage in the group coaching process; it is particularly helpful when the group is finding it challenging to listen to others. Ideally you need to have an even number in the group. I have participated in this to make up numbers, although that does make it more challenging to then coach the group through the process.

What is the process?

1 Ask the coachees to form pairs and in their pairs take a chair each and sit back to back. They should sit far enough away from other pairs so that they don't interfere with the conversations that the other pairs will have.

2 Label one person in the pair A and the other person B.

3 Ask all the As to talk about a subject that both interests them and is important while B listens.

4 Instruct B to listen only without asking any questions, making any sounds or turning round to look at person A.

5 After one minute ask all the As to stop talking.

6 Review what it felt like for the As to talk without any verbal or non-visual cues from person B. Draw out the learning with questions and reflection on what you've heard.

7 Review what it felt like for the Bs to listen without any verbal or non-visual cues from person A. Draw out the learning with questions and reflection on what you've heard.

8 Swap round so person B talks to person A as in Steps 3–7.

9 Ask further questions about how different it was being a talker rather than a listener. What did they notice?

10 Ask them to repeat the exercise from Steps 3–8 but this time the listener is allowed to give verbal cues, such as mms, ahas, yes, oh really. In other words, the listener can demonstrate with short words or sounds that they're listening to the other person.

11 The next step is to add in the asking questions.

12 Repeat the review process as in Steps 6 and 7.

13 Finally, ask them both to sit facing each other and repeat Steps 3–8.

You can flex this process to the amount of time and willingness of the group to keep going. So you could finish it after Step 8. The purpose is to draw out the learning of how they listen and what insights they've had about what they need to do differently. This learning from this exercise can be referred to as the coaching progresses to remind them of the importance of deep-level listening: that is, listening free from judgement and for the benefit of the person talking.

Tool name: magic circle

Tool's purpose

This tool is based on the concept of perceptual positions and focuses the coachees on taking a 360° perspective on a situation. It elicits how well they can put themselves in another's shoes and what they can learn from taking a different view of the issue at hand. The magic element comes from the meta-process of looking above the 360° process and enlisting the help of the group in feeding back what they noticed about the process itself. This is where you can leverage the combined wisdom of the group to give an even broader perspective of what might be happening.

When do I use it?

This is a great tool to use when coachees are experiencing challenging inter-personal situations. The benefit of using this in the group is that you can draw parallels and create thinking space for how the group relates to each other. There are layers of subtlety with this tool that, if allowed to percolate, trigger realizations about what it's like for someone else to experience how you communicate and connect with them. It works best when there are two people involved in the situation: the coachee and the person they're having a challenge with. I ask the main protagonist to really associate with the person they are being, so when they take on the perspective of the other person or the objective bystander, I really want them to imagine what it's like, how the person sits/stands/looks/sounds and so on. You are asking them to act as if they are that person. You will need to allow for emotional as well as rational responses to this tool. Sometimes, the very act of taking on the mantle of someone else triggers a visceral response, and your role as the coach is to make sure the space is as safe as possible and keep a vigilant eye for the individual's and group's safety. It is useful to ask the person who is working with the process to go only where they feel safe. Ensure they know that they can stop the process if at any stage they feel it's becoming too uncomfortable.

In a group coaching scenario it is better to demonstrate the process with a real live situation and then ask the other coachees to work together in pairs using the same process. The process outlined below can be copied by the other coachees as they work together in pairs. Or, if you wish and time allows, you could ask each coachee to go through the process in the larger group. This is one of those situations where the group will know what will work best for them.

What is the process?

1 Ask for someone to step forward who is maybe encountering challenges in a relationship and would like to gain different perspectives on what might be happening and how they can work differently with that person.

2 Explain that you will be asking them to work with each other in the group after having watched how the process works.

3 Ask the coachee who has volunteered to describe the situation from their perspective. What's the situation? How does it make them feel? What has the other person done, said, not done, not said and so on. Really get under the skin of the situation and elicit a real representation from the coachee about what it's like for them.

4 After they've shared as much as they want, ask them to stand up or move around and shake off. You might ask them a question unrelated to what they've just told you or make a joke with them about something unrelated. The aim is to get them physically in a different place ready to take on the next role in this scenario.

5 Once they've shaken off the vestiges of the conversation, ask them to sit or stand in a different place and take on the mantle of the person they were describing so that they 'become' the other person. Find out the other person's name and ask them the questions using that person's name.

6 Ask them what the situation is like from this person's perspective. How do they see the situation? How does it make them feel? Really get under the skin of what it's like from this person's perspective.

7 Follow Step 4.

8 Now that you've heard both perspectives, this time you want them to look at what's happening in the scenario from a dissociated position. Ask them to move to a different place in the room where they can see the situation that's been described by the two characters.

9 Explore this helicopter perspective with them. What have they heard and seen? What is their take on that? What might be really happening in this relationship? What could they both do differently?

10 Finally, ask the group how they experienced the scenario. What did they notice? What might they add? What suggestions do they have? Keep going until all observations, thoughts and ideas naturally run out.

When the group have observed these experiences invite them to work in pairs, following the same process. Allow plenty of time for this process, and when all pairs have finished bring them back together as a combined group for a final review of the learning, insights, challenges, surprises and anything else that came out of the process.

Decision making

Tool name: Cartesian box

Tool's purpose

To help the coachees evaluate decisions and stimulate all aspects of the thinking process. This process is one of the staple coaching tools and most coaches will be familiar with it.

When do I use it?

Sometimes a group gets stuck in a downward spiral of not being able to make decisions. It might even be that they are stuck about what to do next as a group. Not being able to see the wood for the trees sometimes happens when there is so much choice that even the act of making the choice requires a decision. This easy-to-use tool can be used with the combined group or working in smaller groups. There are many ways to use it. I have found that using the space in the room and getting coachees to walk around answering the questions changes their physiology, which releases their mind to work on the questions. Moving around is a metaphor for getting mentally unstuck and so I like to work with the whole group at once. The choice is yours.

What is the process?

1 Write out the four individual questions listed below on four large pieces of paper, one question per piece of paper. You can stick pieces of flipchart paper together to make them bigger, or use rolls of lining paper or brown wrapping paper stuck together.

   a What would you get if you did (topic on which decision is required)?

   b What would you get if you didn't (topic on which decision is required)?

   c What wouldn't you get if you did (topic on which decision is required)?

   d What wouldn't you get if you didn't (topic on which decision is required)?

2 Put each piece of paper in a different part of the room. So in corner A you might have Question a, in corner B you might have Question b, and so on. You can use variants on these questions using the same logic. Use the space available in the room to create different zones for each question.

3 Ask the coachees to work their way around the room and ask them to write their answers using big chunky pens. You and the group decide how they would like to do this: whether they all do it sequentially, or whether half the group starts with a and the other half with d, or they just visit each question as they feel. Typically, in a one-to-one coaching session you would start with a and work through sequentially. Sometimes it helps to mix it up as it interrupts typical thinking habits.

4 Bring the group together and review what's come up.

The added value of this tool comes in the discussion afterwards and your coaching of the group as a whole about the decision-making process. The double-negative questions usually require the greatest brain power, and it is fascinating to watch and listen as the question lands in the coachees' minds. By the end of the discussion, the decision will hopefully be made.

Change and transition

Tool name: bridging the change

Tool's purpose

I am constantly amazed and humbled by the willingness of individuals to step up in a group situation. This tool is based on the brilliant work of William Bridges (hence the name), and works with the transitions we make when encountering changing events around us. Sometimes the most ordinary changes elicit the greatest emotion, and sharing this within the group has power and evokes strong emotional bonds with others in the group.

When do I use it?

This is particularly useful when coachees are experiencing the uncertainty of change. It is also a useful mechanism to engage individuals with the group process and helps creates bonds across and through the group. The very act of disclosing sometimes deeply personal experiences is when this tool comes into its own. It's a great way of gauging which stage the group is at in its maturity.

What is the process?

1 Ask the group to think of a situation when they've personally experienced change. They can choose what they share, and only have to share what they are willing to be out there in the public domain. They choose what they are comfortable disclosing and ask the group to listen with open minds and hearts.

2 Provide the coachees with lots of Post-it notes, chunky pens, flipchart paper and Blu-Tack.

3 Draw three lines on a piece of flipchart paper diagonally as in Figure 8.2. Label the first one, 'Letting go', the middle one 'No man's land' and the third one 'New beginnings'.

FIGURE 8.2

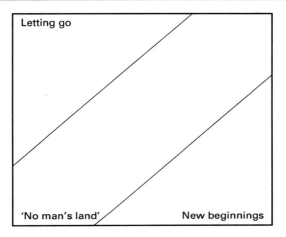

4 Explain what each phase is about. So, the 'Letting go' phase is about the grieving process they experienced for the old way of being, doing and working. The 'No man's land' is the emotional phase of what they experienced, both the upsets of not knowing what was likely to happen and the excitement of something different. This 'No man's land' recognizes that we will have mixed emotions about the change. Some of these will be sad emotions and some will be happy. Either way, we will be processing our emotions as we let go of the old and work through this stuff to make way for the new. The final phase, 'New beginnings', includes the experiences that told them they'd made the transition. For example, they might be working in a different way without realizing it, or they might be using different words without realizing it or the new 'things' don't feel new anymore. In other words, they've integrated the change into their usual daily routine.

5 Ask them to work individually and, using the three headings, jot down one thought per Post-it of what happened during each of these phases.

6 Give them sufficient time to think and capture those experiences. Don't crowd them as they're doing this and be around if they want to share or ask you questions.

7 When they're ready, ask them to draw the diagram on their piece of flipchart and put the Post-its in the relevant phase.

8 Bring the group together and ask for a volunteer to share.

9 Seek input from other members of the group about what they've heard. Ask questions to understand more about the process of transition the person experienced – checking that they are comfortable answering the questions. They can choose whether they wish to answer or not.

10 When they have reached the end ask if anyone else wishes to share their transition.

11 Bring the discussion to a close by seeking feedback on what they're taking away from the exercise and the discussion. Maybe soliciting input on how the process felt – what was it like revisiting that change? What surprised them? What insights do they now have? What have they learned about themselves? How can they apply what they've learned?

The group will only go where they feel safe going, and this tool works really well when you contract for it being ok for coachees to answer and discuss in the group only what is comfortable for them. Some change can be traumatic, and sometimes we might not always be aware of this until we look back and examine what happened. It is humbling to share another's experience of how they've worked through changes, and my experience of using this tool in this way is that it creates a different energy in the room. You immediately know if a group has bonded by the level of disclosure and support shown. How deep the coachees are willing to go in seeking responses to the different phases also indicates their level of self-awareness. Answers that focus on the logical, critical thinking part of the mind indicate both personality preference and willingness to stretch the comfort zone. How you use the process and adapt it to your needs will also reflect your own experiences of change and transition. This is likely to be part of the parallel processing that inevitably occurs in group coaching situations.

- Potential fears/concerns: how can they be handled?
- Potential obstacles/hurdles: how can they overcome?
- What's not OK to bring into the session? What's OK to bring into the session?
- What are you holding inside about the coaching?
- What's happening for you at the moment that might be 'with you' as we work together – positive and negative?
- What might get in the way of us working together?

- How might we handle potential conflicts/disagreements?

- What special 'gifts' when you're at your best do you have to bring to the group? How might we best use these 'gifts'?

Some of these tools address the transactional nature of group coaching – finding answers on 'how to'. Other tools are more transformational and seek to discover what's lying beneath the surface ready to use as a resource for personal growth and development. There is a time and place for both, depending on what the purpose of the coaching is. Each session will differ and the group's maturity plays a part in where the group takes you: transactional or transformational. This is no different from individual coaching. Trust comes into play with the group when working on challenging topics; it's sometimes easier to stick with the task-based stuff rather than go into the sometimes less tangible values, beliefs, attitudes and assumptions territory. The group will only go where they feel safe to go, and your role is to create enough safety for them to explore what they need at the time they need it. So back to your first and most important tool: judgement.

Mastery is deeply rooted in practising the right things, as compared with expertise, which is about reaching a standard. It is also true that sometimes the simpler the tool, the more effective the route to learning. The right tools are the ones that bring the most or best benefits for your coachees. There is no universal definition of what is the right tool because the context and content determines so much. The only right tool you need for your group coaching is sound judgement. Knowing what intervention to make, and when, comes with patience and practice. Discovery is part of the fun of coaching and you will create a curiosity for learning so that even the 'wrong' tool becomes an opportunity for growth – so long as you contract for experimentation. Stay curious about what makes tools tick and use judgement without being judgemental. Tools can land differently with different groups and that's usually an opportunity to learn.

09 Creative group coaching

How do you feel about letting go and just being there for your group? Spend a few minutes exploring this, noticing the feelings that emerge, the images that come to mind and the 'little voice' in your head. Maybe you heard 'Whoa!' or perhaps you felt a surge of energy in your stomach. And maybe you heard 'Yes, that's what coaching is about!' as you imagined yourself sitting with a group just being there as they explore. And maybe you experienced, heard and saw something completely different. This concept of letting go and being completely present lies at the heart of egoless coaching and provides a ready-made pathway for finding creativity. Creativity takes many forms, and tapping into that rich resource of ideas, different perspectives, insights and experimentation means letting go of previously held expectations and the 'shoulds' that permeate our daily lives. Letting go of the need for perfection is a prerequisite for creativity. There is a difference between seeing creativity as a journey and seeking it as a destination. Encouraging your group to tap into their own creativity is a great way to help them focus on solutions rather than problems. It's also a great way of shifting perspectives and freeing up energy and releasing tension.

Einstein and Edison both said they learnt more from the things that didn't work than the things that did (Dweck, 2012), and that spirit of experimentation is a gift for the group coach to open and enjoy. Let's assume that you have already created a solid contract with your group, they know in broad terms what they want to do, be or have from the session, and they are willing to experience and let in those creative forces that each of us has; they might be expressed in a different way but we all have the potential to create. With that foundation on which to build, how will you manifest your creativity in working with that group? Asking people to be creative as they stare blindly at a blank piece of paper is a tough challenge, so let's turn to the work of Howard Gardner (1983) on multiple intelligences. You can use these general headings to provide a great starting point from which to identify how you might work creatively with a group:

- how other people feel;
- how you notice your own feelings;
- logic and numbers;
- music, sound, rhythms;
- physical movement;
- images and spatial awareness;
- words and language.

The following ideas are just that – ideas to help ignite your creative spark and set you free from the shackles of 'perfection'; just do it, enjoy it and review it, then apply the learning.

How other people feel

Group coaching provides an additional benefit over one-to-one coaching because the group becomes a resource for you and the coachees to use and leverage to help with the developmental process. You can be as creative as you feel comfortable with in the way you and the group work together to optimize this benefit. One of the experiences I had many years ago was of the 'mastermind' technique expounded in Napoleon Hill's seminal book (1937). In fact, a variant of this technique is used in Action Learning groups. Having used it many times since, I have noticed and commented on how each time the group adapts the process in a way that makes sense to them. All of the timings, 'rules' and the process can therefore be flexed to suit requirements and needs. Here is the broad process for you to adapt and experiment with.

- Purpose: to harness the collective wisdom of the group and bring into awareness our unconscious resources.
- Objective: the group will coach one person to increase their awareness and resources around a topic/challenge/issue so that they are able to take action.

What is the process?

1 One person volunteers to be the coachee; the group then becomes the coach. It is useful for the coachee to have a pen and paper ready to hand to jot down information that is particularly useful for them.

2 There are other roles that need to be performed: observer, timekeeper and process monitor. If the group wish to allocate these roles among themselves then great. Alternatively, the group may take responsibility for self-monitoring.

3 You as the 'super coach' observe the process and provide 'expertise' as required – you may also participate, depending on the wishes of you and the group.

4 The group decides how long they wish to spend on each activity.

5 The coachee states their challenge/issue/topic within the allocated timeframe.

6 After hearing what the coachee has to say, there is a specified time for each 'coach' to have an opportunity to ask questions of clarification. Typically this step is about clarifying the most pertinent points for the benefit of the coachee, not the coach! In other words, this is summary and reflection through questioning.

7 The next step is about identifying resources that the coachee already has: that is, what the coaches have noticed that is positive and useful, that the coachee has perhaps missed. It might be something like: 'I noticed that in working with your challenge you've demonstrated great resolve.' Allow the coachee time to jot down any points after each comment.

8 Following on from this, each coach provides their insight and ideas of how the coachee might move forward. At this stage the coachee is only required to thank each coach for their input and note any points that the coachee feels are particularly helpful.

9 Finally, the coachee has the opportunity to feedback to the group of coaches what insights, help, surprises and any other comments about what has come out from the session.

After the process has been completed the 'super coach' (ie you) helps the group dissect the session, take an overview of the process and draw out what was happening for the coachee volunteer and the coachees as the process emerged. There are different levels of learning and coaching when using this technique, and the coach should also ensure that they discuss the process itself: what did the group like, dislike, learn, feel? What did they notice about what was coming up for them as the coachee stated their challenge/ issue/topic? What might they do differently next time? This feedback can be used to develop the process into one that the group owns and can use again. You can repeat the process above for each person within the group if you have a full day's coaching session, or you could take it in turns with a different person in the coachee position at each session and mix it up with other coaching activities. I like to spend as long on this review activity as the process itself. This is also part of the group coaching activity because you are bringing into awareness the unconscious resource within the group. A realization, for example, that the topic evokes an emotional response from one of the coachees is a great jumping-off point to discuss what's happening and how this might be experienced in the 'real world'; the triggers that create a 'click-whirr' response in us without us being consciously aware.

The value of the group is in its collective wisdom, and another tool that is really helpful at tapping into how other people feel is the 'Stop, start, continue' feedback tool. This is probably a tool to use when the group is already on its journey together. Finding out how each individual's behaviour impacts others is helpful feedback from both an individual and group developmental perspective. It will require strict ground rules about how the tool is to be used within the group, and these should come from the group itself. It will require of the coachees an open mind and open ears and a focus on listening with a view to learn rather than judge. It works best when they can be free from judgement about both the feedback they receive and the responses it evokes in them. In other words, they should allow their vulnerability to emerge with a view to learning something new about themselves. How they choose to use that information is then up to them. The tool is simple and straightforward and can be facilitated in many different ways. One way is to ask each member of the group to provide feedback for each of their coaching colleagues under the headings: Stop, Start, Continue. They can write up this feedback before the session so that time during the session is spent giving the feedback with the notes as an aid to memory. Where a group has a high level of maturity, ask them to provide this feedback in a one-to-one setting where they share their thoughts with each other in pairs and follow the process until they have provided and received feedback from everyone in the group. In other words, they keep swapping partners. The other way of doing this is to collate all the feedback anonymously and provide a written report for each individual, which they then discuss in pairs or as a whole group – depending on the maturity level and trust within the group.

Encouraging the group to talk about what's happening in the group process ultimately refers back to how people feel – they may not express it as such and your role is to help surface what's going on so that it be brought into the room and used as a resource for learning and growth. Sometimes, a simple drawing exercise about the 'process so far' can act as a catalyst for deeper discussion and exploration. Similarly, all of these exercises can be used to elicit how people feel in relation to the coachee's specific coaching topic. For example, if they are encountering challenges with a work colleague, asking them to draw how their work colleague might feel will bring to the surface some of the more tangential aspects of the relationship and how the coachee views it. You could also use images from magazines that the coachee uses to create a collage of what's happening for other people in that relationship. Our internal representation of reality is often expressed in metaphor; these tools help that process.

Our first stepping-off point in creative coaching tools suggests that you don't have to do anything wacky or outrageous to express creativity – it's about taking tools and techniques that you are already familiar with and tailoring them for a group scenario.

How you notice your own feelings

Noticing how other people feel is one half of the equation; the other half is noticing your own feelings and being aware of what's happening for you in the moment. A tool that is particularly helpful is Johari's Window (Figure 9.1), which will be familiar to most coaches. The tool was created by Joseph Luft and Harry Ingham in 1950. The idea behind the tool is that we have a window through which we see the world and the world sees us. How much we see and allow others to see is determined by our level of self-awareness and awareness of others:

FIGURE 9.1

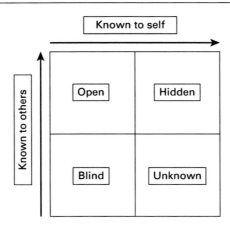

- Open – both seen by us and others.

- Hidden – only seen by us, and kept secret from others.

- Blind – how others see us but of which we are unaware.

- Unknown – untravelled territory – an opportunity to explore.

There are a number of ways to use this in a group coaching setting and you will know which will work for the group based on your knowledge and feel for what's happened so far in the group. It goes without saying that trust and willingness to allow vulnerability in the relatively safe environment of the group coaching sessions will determine the results – positive and/or negative. Each type, though, is an opportunity for growth and it is down to the skill of the coach to create the safe space to explore.

The tool was originally based on 56 adjectives and feedback solicited from others as well as the individual. They were all invited to tick which adjectives best described the individual. Where there was agreement on the adjective, it was recorded in the open window; where only the coachee ticked the adjective, it went in the hidden window; where only the respondent ticked the adjective, it went in the blind window; and all other un-ticked adjectives were placed in the unknown window. So, you could ask the group to come up with a list of adjectives by brainstorming, or you could use a ready-made list. Or not use adjectives at all. In true 'egoless' coaching style, simply explaining the purpose of the exercise and inviting the group to create a process for how they will use it together is even better. In co-creating the process they will have created trust and be more open to sharing vulner-ability and learning.

Another way of using this tool is to create a physical 'window' on the floor – you could ask each coachee to create their own window and use it as an opportunity to invite other coachees to share with them their thoughts about them in the open and blind window and for the coachee to share with them their hidden window. They could then work together to explore what might be behind the unknown window. This process approach allows the coachee to choose someone they trust most within the group to share their 'window'. Clearly, if one coachee is requested many times, this will impact the timing of the session. So, plan up front with the group who they wish to have in their window and work out the logistics together as a group.

One way of tracking progress is to share the window in Figure 9.2 to demonstrate how the panes of glass might have grown during the coaching process. And also explore with the coachees how they now experience the window at the end of the coaching sessions compared with when they first did the exercise. As the coach, being creative and free from the need to demonstrate expertise in the tool, allows the coachees to experiment with this tool in a way which works for them. Let go of any need to 'get it right' and allow the process to emerge and work, since ultimately this is all about self-awareness and disclosure. As a developmental tool for the coach, it might be worth noticing what comes up for you when you coach others in this process. Often this exercise triggers 'stuff' that is going on for us as the coach and this is a useful discussion point for supervision and self-reflection.

FIGURE 9.2

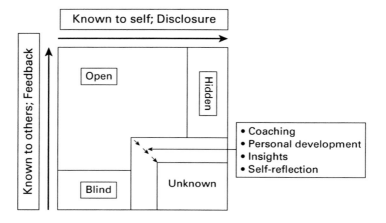

Logic and numbers

You will probably have noticed that the different intelligence 'types' also correlate to personality preferences, and this category of logic and numbers will both play to the interests of those coachees with this preference type and also stretch those of a different type. I am a huge fan of quizzes and have to confess that I do use 'rewards' in some of my group activities for those who score highly. It makes it fun and adds a bit of frisson in the group, which in turn creates energy. It is not helpful to create too much competition but just enough to push the coachees out of their comfort zone and the sometimes hypnotic trance they can enter when listening to others speak! The content of the quizzes will be determined by the content of the coaching and you can be as creative as you like with the questions you ask – it must make sense to the coachees and test their learning so far.

For those with a numbers bias, you could introduce elements of business planning into the sessions that focus on working out the numerical consequence of actions identified. For example, asking them to identify in monetary terms the value they're getting from coaching is an interesting exercise. One way of approaching this is to find out how much their current situation is costing them; we very rarely think about the monetary cost of our activities. You could then ask them to think about the monetary implications of how moving forward from their current position to their desired state will impact them. This could be done in the group wide setting – allowing people to fire off thoughts from each other.

One of my personal favourites in this category is the Cartesian logic questioning outlined in the previous chapter:

1 What would happen if you did [do, be, have XYZ]?

2 What would happen if you didn't [do, be, have XYZ]?

3 What wouldn't happen if you did [do, be, have XYZ]?

4 What wouldn't happen if you didn't [do, be, have XYZ]?

The process for using this with the group is down to your own creativity. To recap, one way I have used it is to put each question in relation to the specific decision on a piece of flipchart paper. Each flipchart is positioned in a different part of the room and the coachees are asked to visit each question in turn starting with Question 1. They write their answers on Post-it notes and put their initials in the corner so that they can be reviewed later. When all questions have been visited the group comes together to discuss the input. Clearly this only works for one topic, so this has to be a topic that the group wants to come to a decision on together.

Another way of using this tool is to ask coachees to work on their own topics individually first of all (thus you will need four pieces of flipchart paper per coachee), and then work in pairs or threes, to discuss what has come up. Each coachee will swap around so that one shares their input whilst the other(s) listen and provide feedback and insights.

Venn diagrams are great ways of representing conflicting interests in situations; you could use children's hoola-hoops to represent the different parties/situations and ask coachees to step into the hoops to describe their perspective and explore what the areas of overlap might be (Figure 9.3) Again, this is something they could work on in pairs or threes rather than the whole group. If the topic/situation is common to all coachees, then this could be used with the whole group.

FIGURE 9.3

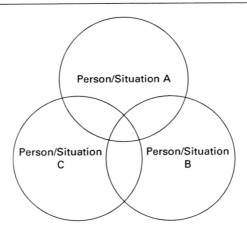

Images and spatial awareness

This is about using the space and environment in a creative way – in other words not necessarily how it was intended. For example, how can you use the chairs and tables to create a physical metaphor for the coaching experience? Could you use yoga mats and ask people to sit on the floor for some sessions? Experimenting with the physical space snaps people out of their psychological habits – you know what this is like. On workshops it's usual that people will sit in the same chair, next to the same person. By creating uncertainty in the physical layout you free up the mental space for thinking and doing in a different way. Note that your coachees may well find this uncomfortable, and the trick is not to shy away from moving them gradually out of their comfort zone. In some sessions you might have a 'traditional' room layout and in others a less conventional approach. The room itself becomes a resource for you to use to create a physical space in which to experience and experiment.

One of the NLP tools that works well with space is Neurological Levels, developed by Robert Dilts. In fact you could create different 'labels' and ask people to walk through them, experiencing, seeing and hearing what they hear when they're in that state. An example of this could be emotional states such as 'happiness', 'success', 'setbacks' and so on. Listen to the words that your coachees use to describe their experiences and use this to draw on. You could approach this by asking people to move to a different place in the room that represents a particular feeling. Then ask them to move to another part of the room that represents a different state, and to explore how and in what way that space is different.

We've already talked about how you might use images and drawing; in addition you might want to use modelling clay and ask people to 'sculpt' a physical representation of their issue/topic and use that as a springboard to create other 'sculptures'. That act of making something physical changes the way we perceive it and leads to different perspectives and insights that hitherto have been unknown or hidden. Painting is also a great way of releasing creative tension – the use of colour, texture and sheer delight in just 'playing'. We are so often required to switch into 'adult' thinking mode that we forget our creativity and ability to create solutions comes from the natural child. Anything you can do as the coach to create a playful environment will encourage the coachees that it's ok to just play and see what comes up. Very often the results can be surprising, not necessarily because of the specific 'things' that the coachees create but the meanings they attach.

Music, sound rhythms

As a musician I am fully aware of the benefits of music in the creative process. The use of music to evoke mood and diffuse tension is well known, and recent research suggests that music stimulates emotional centres in the brain. Lorna McDowell shared how she uses music at the beginning of sessions to help quieten the mind so that the coachees are present in the moment and able to tap into their stream of consciousness. In another way, Angela mentioned that the different speed, tone and pace of the voice help coachees access the questions at a deeper level. Think about how you could introduce music, sound and rhythm into the coaching sessions.

Music experienced in groups can be a deeply moving experience and help bond the group in a 'tribal' way. Many years ago at a corporate conference we were initiated to the benefit of drums. There were around 250 people in the room and as we each beat out the same rhythm in unison the vibrations started to connect with our upper body area. It was interesting to observe how these typically reserved individuals suddenly started to smile and loosen up. You could use a similar technique with tambourines, or just clapping your hands in rhythm. To keep the brain engaged, use different rhythm patterns to keep people on their toes. Once you have a steady flow then you could perhaps ask people to verbalize in one word how they're feeling. This might be a great introduction to the session and hopefully create a few laughs to release some energy and endorphins so that you're ready to be creative together and come up with some fantastic solutions-based thinking and being.

If you're reading this and starting to feel the slightest bit uncomfortable – perhaps because you're not musical – don't worry. This isn't about being a musician, it's about providing a conduit for the coachees to have an experience that they wouldn't normally have in their day-to-day activities. Let go of the need to be 'right' and just enjoy the experience – find out what happens and then use that to generate a discussion about how it felt. There will probably be coachees who feel uncomfortable with some of this and might even think it silly. That's a great point at which to initiate a discussion about 'shoulds' and conventional ways of being and what that might mean for their beliefs – and where those beliefs come from.

This is an area where you can really have fun and experiment; even simple things like asking people to bring in a piece of text – poetry or prose – and read to the group out loud. You can experiment with how words sound when you give them different emphasis. You could even ask people to 'act out' certain passages and notice how their breathing and internal processes kick in. When singing I create a mental movie of the piece I'm singing, which I then relive in the moment as I sing. The internal process of singing becomes the enjoyment piece because I am fully present in my body and with the experience. Drawing out learning from simple things such as this is where the joy of working with groups becomes apparent; you never know exactly what to expect and each time you have the gift of surprise.

Physical movement

This aspect is partly covered in spatial awareness and builds on clean language tools. One way you might use this is by adapting the GROW model:

- Goal – What do they want? What is their outcome from the coaching?
- Reality – What is happening right now? What have they done already to reach their goal/outcome?
- Options – What could they do if there were no barriers? What if they had a magic wand?
- Will or wrap up – How committed are they to their goal? What actions are they going to take and when?

So you might ask the group to work in a space called 'goals'. They choose where this space is and have to physically stand up and move to that space. They then describe their goal from that space. You will then ask them to move to another space called 'current reality' and ask them to describe this, and so on until you have explored all aspects of the GROW model. Asking the coachees to move around the room to different places that they choose engages a different aspect of their being. This might be a good exercise to do in pairs or threes and rotate roles so that each person has a chance to coach and be coached. If you do it in threes, then the third person could perform the role of an observer and note what they experience, both about the process and the other two people in the group. Sometimes when a group has been sitting for a long time you can feel the energy slowly sapping away as they sink deeper into their seats. At this time it's always a good idea to get people up and moving. A simple exercise such as asking people to swap seats can help – or perhaps you could suggest that they stand up and walk around the room in silence. For those coachees who are particularly at ease with this type of activity, you could ask them to adopt certain poses as they walk around – for example, walk around in a happy way etc.

The next tool is to be used with caution and only where you and the group feel 100 per cent safe and comfortable with each other. For the purist amongst you this tool is based very loosely on a technique known as 'sculpting', which in turn is based on systemic constellations integrated by Bert Hellinger from the work of Virginia Satir. It was originally devised in a therapeutic setting for group family therapy. The way I describe it here is my experience of how I've used it working with groups, and each time has been different but each time has proved to be extremely helpful for the coachee. (And for the other members of the group – as there is always parallel processing at some level.)

Purpose: to help the coachee see the situation/topic 'acted out' so that they can get insight and inspiration from the 'players' and have a different perspective.

Objective: to act out the situation 'as if' the players were the actual people.

1 Set the ground rules for this exercise by checking that everyone in the room is ok with working through this 'play', and by being aware that sometimes there is emotional release when working with this tool. Explain that the intention of using the tool is for coaching purposes only. (In other words it is not a therapy intervention in the coaching setting.)

2 Request that the topics brought to the 'play' are safe and that the coachee presenting the 'play' is ok that they might have an emotional response based on hitherto unknown or unaware 'stuff' that is in their unconscious.

3 Ask the coachee to *briefly* describe the situation, who the key players are and what their key characteristics are – this is to help those members of the group who will play these people to get 'in character'.

4   Ask for other members of the group to volunteer to play the 'characters' in the 'play'.

5   The coachee then positions the 'players' in the scene and asks them to 'act out' the scenario they have described.

6   The coachee may direct the action accordingly.

7   The 'play' may reach a natural conclusion or the coachee can say 'cut'.

8   At the end of the 'play' the coachee feeds back their insights and thoughts and feelings about what they have just experienced. They can also ask the 'players' for their insights as well.

Having been both a facilitator and 'actor' in these activities, it is surprising how readily you assume the role that you have been given and start to experience the emotions and thoughts of the character you are playing. It is therefore absolutely vital at the end of this session you ask everybody to physically shake off the characters and change their state by telling a joke, getting them to laugh or do something different before moving into the next activity. And even with all the setting up and safety notices at the beginning of this tool, you should expect the unexpected. We all carry psychological baggage that is out of our awareness and there is something in this tool that, when we see it played out in front of us, brings to our attention and engages an emotional connection with our unconscious awareness.

Angela Dunbar, master clean language and emergent knowledge coach, explains how she uses movement and visual representations in an online group coaching environment:

Another thing using the online element, at times has been [being] able to use webcam in creative ways. For instance talking through a coach–client relationship, a coachee could actually map out a visual representation of that, with a drawing, diagram or even toy figurines. You need a webcam to take off the laptop. You can move these figurines... in a 3-D model of what it's like. Webcams don't have to be directed at your face. You can have people bring drawings and use the webcams to show people how it's evolved. Webcams are a great way of focusing on a particular aspect of the visual without distractions again... I worked with a coachee who decided they wanted to move during the session, and it was transformational for them, they were walking all around gaining insight standing from different places... they decided they were going to go to the end of their garden and get on a trampoline and jump up and down on the trampoline. And with each jump they were seeing more and more of what was going on around them. They were on a portable handset and we still managed to keep the signal. There were huge insights, it was a demonstration, you could hear in this person's voice. Realizing just by jumping up they could see much further.

Physicality is a key tool for the coach to use and create interesting learning and growth opportunities. Keeping it simple is sometimes a great way to start with this one if you, yourself, are not too comfortable with experimenting in this area. Paying attention to your own physical needs is a great place to begin the awareness process, and listening to what's happening for you when you move around with the group is a resource you can use to bring into the room and start a discussion.

Words and language

There is research (Krizman *et al*, 2012) that suggests that bilinguals are better able to suppress non-relevant stimuli in order to focus their attention on the most relevant data and stay focused. This fascinating research has implications for how we focus attention. Getting creative with words and language provides a means of developing other ways of expressing what's happening and provides different stimuli and helps break old habits. In *50 Top Tools* we outline some phrases and words that we use to give ourselves a negative script. We know that the words we use are imbued with emotion and meaning way beyond their literal interpretation, and in fact our verbal habits are a direct manifestation of how we're processing, interacting and experiencing our world. As a coach, you'll probably have noticed how sometimes just one question will throw the coachee completely because the words you've chosen have deeper significance for them. There are no specific examples here because it literally can be anything – and sometimes the most innocuous questions elicit the strongest response. The research suggests that bilinguals mentally juggle between languages, which in turn focuses their attention in a different way. This suggests that when we use a different or unfamiliar language or words to express questions or thoughts, there is a lower degree of linkage between those unfamiliar words and emotions. This is because we use those words less frequently and therefore have not created the neural pathway that connects the words with the feelings.

How does this help you with coaching your group? You could ask them to record a conversation and note down how many words seem to have negative connotations. You could also do this activity in threes, where one person asks the coachee questions whilst the observer notes down the negative words they notice – or words that seem to carry an emotional energy. Then feedback the words to the coachee and ask them what meaning is attached to those words. For example, 'I noticed that you used the word "try" x number of times; what does "try" mean to you?' Were they aware that they'd formed a verbal habit?

I once coached someone who worked with horses and when they were stuck on how to come up with ideas I asked them what their horse might say. And they immediately whinnied as if they were a horse. They were then able to access what that whinny meant and in the 'horse' persona found a different voice. I have used this in other ways by asking the coachees to find a character that epitomizes the quality or characteristics they want. It is like magic when suddenly they find a different way of speaking and being. We often get stuck in a dead-end language pattern, and finding that chink of light that leads us to a different path just requires us to change words and ways of speaking, or in the case of the horse, whinnying!

A willingness to just go with something that is out of the ordinary and unexpected allows the coachee to access a different part of their brain and circumvent the verbal habits they've created. Sometimes it works, sometimes it doesn't. Courage and freedom from perfection are definitely what is required in this area and a willingness to ask 'what if...?'

Combined intelligences

Creativity in coaching is about combining your total experience and resources in a way that helps move the coachees to a different, hopefully better (but not always) place. Using the ideas here as a starting point to grow your own creativity, think about how you might combine some of these ideas and how you might adapt or change them. Ironically for a chapter on creativity, I started with a structure – the intelligences identified by Howard Gardner. I'd like to invite you put these aside and just 'be' creative in whatever way that makes sense to you. Free from structure and content, how could you unleash your creativity and develop a session that flows from that creative source?

Creativity starts with a growth mindset

Liberating talent from the chains of limiting mindsets is the fundamental purpose of coaching and personal development. Action creates habits and influences mindset; each small step of progress provides the mind with evidence that it is possible to grow and change, and creates a virtuous cycle of thoughts, action, attitude and behaviour. Dweck's notion of the growth mindset is a great place to end this creative session. She talks about the fact that none of us arrives at a position or role perfectly formed – we are works in progress. Our ability to learn and grow comes from a belief that we are all inherently capable of being talented – the difference between potential and actual is down to dogged determination and persistent action and review. My request to you as a coach is to foster this notion that neither you nor your coachees arrive perfectly formed at the first session. The purpose of creativity is to generate something; the very act of creation is about bringing something into being. By adopting this mindset you will hopefully free yourself up from the often all-too-compelling need to be 'expert' and allow both yourself and your coachees the opportunity to grow together.

To coach the group you have first to coach yourself; letting go of your own need for perfection and doing things right is the culmination of the egoless coach's journey. If you've followed the journey in this book you will have established your purpose, process and toolset, and the rest is down to trusting that it works. Creativity has a natural environment in which to flourish.

KEY POINTS

- There is no right or wrong when it comes to being creative – only what works!

- Use the collective energy within the group to spark off each other and encourage experimentation and 'letting go'.

- If it helps, create stepping off points from existing models and theories – but don't be tied to them.

- Creativity requires a little bravery and a lot of faith in the group – trust the group and your process, and always encourage learning.

- Foster a growth mindset in yourself and your coachees and demonstrate your belief that we are all inherently capable of being talented.

PART FOUR
Measuring success

The challenges of measuring results from group coaching

10

This is probably the most controversial topic in the book so far, because here I explore some of the beliefs around measurement and how the law of unintended consequences sometimes means that the results, either positive or negative, are used to demonstrate cause and effect linkage from coaching, when in fact there might not be any link, or only limited linkage, between coaching and the results obtained. That does not mean that there is no benefit from measuring results simply because you can't say for definite that one causes the other. What it does mean is that you need to ensure that the end results have taken into account the starting point. Therefore, it may seem counterintuitive, but ending with the start in mind means taking into account your starting point when assessing the results you obtain through group coaching.

If you are using group coaching as part of your talent management strategy, it is vital that you have a keen understanding both of the component parts of your talent management system and where they fit in the wider organizational system. For instance, you could assess the likely impact on the time, resources and commitment for other activities and how this might impact results. How will group coaching fit with other systems that are already in play? And knowing what you know about the organization, what potential knock-on effects – positive or negative – might come from this? How you view 'talent' within the organization and the impact that group coaching might have on how 'talent' is perceived and treated is something else to consider *before* you embark on your group coaching strategy. Reflection beforehand on the current reality and options available is part of the approach for any talent management intervention. Creating expectations when you have little chance of proving, or at least demonstrating, efficacy will lead to disappointment; because the system itself creates results. Ensuring that your clients take a systemic thinking perspective means that the results they may obtain from the coaching process can be placed in the wider context of that 'system'.

It is also helpful to understand this wider system if you are to measure the on-going success of the coaching. Sometimes coachees' behaviour changes and they start to obtain improved results from this behaviour change. With the passage of time, their behaviour patterns can sometimes slip back to their 'old habits'. By taking a systemic perspective on this set of results you add in variables, such as culture, on individual behaviour. In fact we have already encountered this concept earlier when we explored the notion of social proofing. Ending with the start in mind is about gaining clarity in two ways. First is that you focus on what you know about the 'system' in which the coaching has taken place; and second, you approach any results with caution, taking into account the 'unknown' variables that might have led to their manifestation. What I will do is outline some ways of assessing results that are popular at the moment, such as return-on-investment calculations, and also explore the notion of systemic thinking and our old friend 'purpose'.

Having set the scene for systemic thinking, we shouldn't underestimate the value of measuring success, as this is clearly an important step in the coaching process; if you're using group coaching in an organizational setting, that measurement is probably a key factor in whether or not coaching is continued in the future. Here's the rub about success though: it will be different for everyone involved. Measuring results, on the other hand, is perceived as more straightforward – particularly in a business setting where everything reduces to a number. It is likely you will have measurements of results on both a monetary and non-monetary basis. Clearly there is an assumption that every organization is focused primarily on return on investment, and this may or may not be the case. Based on my own experience, asking an organization to clarify exactly what they're expecting from the coaching generates answers ranging from the unknown to the crystal clear. As a group coach your task is to elicit how everyone will measure success and how the results will be measured. This means understanding what will be measured and how. One of the most illuminating questions to ask at the end of the coaching assignment is: looking back at where we started, is this where you expected to be at the end of this process? Other questions that might unlock wisdom about where those results derive are:

- Knowing what you know now, both about yourself and the situation or organization, what factors do you think have been at play in realizing these results?

- What other factors could have influenced these results?

Sometimes taking that backward perspective brings into the present all the learning and insights that the coachee has experienced along the way. Sometimes it doesn't. What I'd like to do is take you on a journey of how everything we've covered so far brings you to this point of measurement, and why at the start of the journey you should take into account all factors, not just the ones that are given to you by your sponsor client, or individual client.

Legacy, vision, strategy

Let's return to the beginning of our journey and revisit purpose. In organizational terms this is at the heart of vision and mission. It's the reason why the organization exists and the purpose it seeks to enact. For individual clients, it's their dream or ideal image, story or state that they wish to attain from the coaching *and* why that's important for them. In NLP terms this is the 'chunking up' process to arrive at the highest value for this vision. This is the starting point for measuring the results from coaching. Ultimately this is the reason why coaching is deployed rather than some other method. Let's do a recap on what is meant by legacy, vision and strategy.

Legacy

The origins of this word are found in the inheritance laws, where a legacy was a bequest in a will or a gift. This is about how the deceased wished to be remembered to those they left behind. I describe this as the energy footprint you create when you leave the room. You can't control it because it's a perception. The only thing that you can control is how you act and behave. In organizational terms this is the impact that an organization has on society, the environment, employees and others that its business activities influence and impact. For individuals this is about how you affect other people by your presence. Reputation in the broadest sense underpins legacy.

Vision

There is the apocryphal story of the two stonemasons working on a building, chipping away at a block of stone. They are asked what they are doing and one replies, 'I'm making a brick for this building' and the other says 'I'm helping to build a cathedral.' This simple story outlines what vision is about; it's the purpose beyond and above the mundane.

Strategy

The word strategy comes from ancient Athens where generals, *strategoi*, directed the activities of the army and navy to achieve success in battle. Strategy is about what plans you put in place to help realize your vision; it is a plan for bringing your future vision to fruition. Your strategy serves your vision, and how it is deployed helps create your legacy. It provides focus for your time and resource and is something you can measure progress against.

Measuring a number happens at a fixed point – it's about something that's happened and has now been realized. So it tells you the 'what' but not the 'why' or 'how' it happened. So if you're going to measure a number at the end of the coaching process, it is essential to allow your clients an opportunity to discover what lies beneath that outcome, why it is important to them and what bigger purpose it serves. For some clients, the coaching outcome is simply to find that purpose as they lack clarity around purpose. These coachees typically repeat patterns of saying: 'I don't know.' Sometimes it's because they genuinely don't know because there is too much choice, and other times it's because that 'not knowing' is symptomatic of lack of purpose. In Viktor Frankl's seminal book *Man's Search for Meaning* (1959) he outlines powerfully the reason why purpose is a fundamental driver for our existence. One of the simple tools I outlined earlier was around helping clients visualize their outcome, and certainly this tool can be helpful as part of this process. There is also a more fundamental aspect of how obtaining that outcome contributes to recognizing what's important for that individual and/or organization. The other aspect of that starting point is therefore the legacy that the coaching activity seeks to fulfil. In practical terms, this is the individual's and organization's context for why they do what they do. Here are some suggested questions that might help elucidate further what was in mind at the start of the process:

- Through this coaching process, what have you discovered about what this means for you/your organization?

- When you started this process what was important to you/your organization?
- What is important to you now?
- If this has changed, what's the reason for that change?
- What was your purpose?
- How has coaching helped further your purpose?
- Where are you now, in relation to your purpose?

It can be easy to focus on the component parts and get into the detail of measurement; however, unless you understand why you're measuring something it's all a bit pointless. The first step to ending with the start in the mind is to switch to a data not numbers mindset. This means that the numbers are useful indicators of how things are moving in a particular direction, but they don't necessarily tell you how to continue or change that movement unless you take a holistic view.

The system you start with influences results

I've used the words system and systemic thinking without really defining them, and I offer lay definitions free from academic jargon. A system is:

> a collection of interconnected processes, mechanisms, beliefs, actions, behaviours and assumptions grouped and defined by the context in which they operate. For example, in an organization, the management system relates to how the business is managed; in everyday life, families are a system in which we interact and play a role.

Culture is definitely a system, and regardless of whether you are coaching people in organizations or outside the work sphere, they will no doubt be part of a particular culture and this will be a factor in what perspective they take on the coaching experience.

Systemic thinking is:

> a holistic view of how something works/operates.

If you are using group coaching to leverage talent in an organization, then the concept of systemic thinking is crucial in appreciating the effects of 'culture' on behaviour and how (or if) this has impacted the results the group has obtained. For example, aggressive and competitive cultures are likely to create behaviour patterns that differ from cultures that are collaborative and supportive of learning. Although coaching might work in both, the basis on which it is measured and the way it is experienced will also be different. The holistic view mentioned earlier pertains to a belief that the sum of the parts is greater than the whole: in other words, that there is a value in connecting individuals together and their combined energy will create more benefit. This synthesis view can be applied to groups of coachees forming part of the bigger group in which they operate, be it organization, family or society as a whole.

Understanding the reason for coaching and arriving at the core purpose therefore only makes sense when taken in this wider context, or system. Remember the example given by Lorna of the challenge she and a colleague had with two coachees who were parallel processing the acquisition process of businesses in the group coaching sessions. Their open dislike and conflict with one another was a direct consequence of the system in which they were working.

> As flies to wanton boys are we to the gods, they kill us for their sport (William Shakespeare, *King Lear*).

The above quote, remembered from my school days, captures this notion of how we are all subject to a system at an unconscious level. When coachees undertake a coaching assignment they expect changes (as do their sponsors or other stakeholders such as family members), but if they go back into the same system you will almost inevitably see the old behaviours creep back in. Group coaching without purpose may increase the individual's and that particular group's performance *but* they are not free from the influences of the wider system. That system might be the organization or social situation or personal circumstance the group or individual is in. One of the key challenges of measuring results in coaching or any 'soft skills' development is that it's problematic to pick out cause and effect. Individuals live in complex social environments and systems, so assessing results is not a science as not all parameters can be controlled and accounted for. The interrelationships on which systems depend for their survival also provide succour for behaviours that keep the system alive, and lead to disdain for those behaviours that do not! Your mission as the group coach is to be vigilant to the whole system and be mindful that you are only experiencing one aspect of the coachees' reality.

When it comes to measuring the results of the coaching, there are a number of factors to be aware of and ensure have been taken into account. As an aside, one programme I managed many years ago achieved fantastic results: that is to say, the numbers were great. As a systemic thinker I did wonder how much had changed in the system in order to deliver the numbers and how much had been down to some of these factors I mention below.

The law of unintended consequences

This can be both a negative or positive consequence. So the attribution theory suggests that we ascribe blame or praise to individuals or groups based on the results they've achieved, when in fact their actions were inconsequential to the results. Cost cutting is just one of these activities, and organizations often ascribe great achievements to one thing when in fact a number of factors combined to create that result.

Focus on the numbers as a definite fact of change

When there is a big number involved or the bigger picture is the driving force – for example when the business is struggling in a tough climate, or a certain number is set as a target – people invariably ignore conflicting data or even ignore data full stop. Receiving a defined customer-satisfaction rating is great news but when you start to look at the wider commercial context, attaining that number year on year might be an indicator that something is getting worse not better compared with the system in which it operates.

The degree of attention that particular subject receives

When you pay attention to something, the filters you operate are tuned in to a different frequency, meaning that data hitherto unimportant suddenly come into your awareness and that very act imbues them with importance. Once you start to focus on something your actions automatically divert to that focus. So it might not be the specific actions you are taking that cause the result; rather, the fact that now you are giving it the required attention so that you take action. Your role as a group coach is to be mindful of boundaries within the group coaching process and at the same time understand that group coaching is not an isolated activity. It takes place in a context that is influenced by and affects other parts of that context. The coaching process continues long after the coach has left the building!

Results = feedback

The results you and your coachees obtain are data points: feedback on which a choice can be exercised. Do you change course or steer in the same direction? We've established that group coaching is a process and a set of behaviours; the same is true of measurement. Return on Investment (ROI) is one of the key measures used by organizations to assess whether or not an investment has been worthwhile. It is, however, only one measure, and group coaching is ultimately about creating organizational wisdom for the future so that talent at all levels can be developed, deployed and engaged. We all have our own ways of measuring worth and there are implications for focusing only on ROI. Organizations with a mindset that sees results as data to use and help assess actions to establish whether they are potentially worth pursuing will see ROI as only one measure. Sustained results require time and energy – they require constancy of purpose to pursue improvement. Improvement only comes with:

- Repetition.
- Purposeful practice.
- Creating new habits.
- Acting – mindset-action. Mindset change starts with action. Repetition gets it into the muscle memory.

If you only adopt an ROI mindset, it suggests that the task is done once the calculation is complete. Far better to take a Return on Worth (ROW) and Return on Growth (ROG) calculation. This suggests that continual growth provides return and is on-going rather than a fixed point, and makes it worth pursuing as part of a wider talent management strategy. If you adopt a learning mindset to all activities then you will always get a return. At the beginning of this chapter I noted that measurement is a black art because hidden behind the pseudo-science of ROI is a belief-set that results are finite and always objective – after all, numbers don't lie! ROI is increasingly coming under scrutiny simply because of some of the factors we've discussed already around 'the system' and systemic thinking versus pure cause and effect. In a coaching context, results are just feedback – to be used or discarded through intelligent choice and hopefully in the pursuit of continuing personal development. To help understand how you might measure ROI to help create a Return on Growth (ROG) let's dive into how it's calculated.

Return on investment explained

To help understand how ROI calculation works there are certain factors that specifically need to be identified and assigned a value:

- initial investment;
- specific quantified changes from the coaching – both expected and observed;
- quantified impact of the changes to the working activities of the coachees – both expected and observed;
- the movement of the change ie increased, reduced, maintained;
- measured over time, ie at least 12 months.

Most coaches will now be familiar with *The Manchester Review* article (McGovern *et al*, 2001) that outlined this calculation. Put simply, improvements gained through group coaching need to be disaggregated from other unrelated improvements and then adjusted for the level of certainty we have that coaching has led to this improvement and an assessment of the overall accuracy of the figures. Here's a shortened explanation of how the calculation works. Let's imagine that the initial group coaching investment for six coachees has been £30,000. For each coachee this investment is £5,000. At the end of the group coaching sessions one of the coachees has increased their delegation activities and strategic thinking – they're now actively managing the delegation process using a systematic approach (ie planned and organized), and this has freed up time for them to focus on more strategic long-term activities. Keeping things simple lets work through a potential calculation:

> Let's assume for this one coachee there has been an improvement in sales of £114,000. However, other changes have taken place during this period which would have led to increased sales whether or not coaching had taken place. So let's assume that 50% of the improvement is due to coaching. This leads to an improvement of £57,000. We then consider the certainty of this figure and its accuracy. In this case we are 100% certain that this figure is solely attributable to coaching and 95% certain that this figure rings true. Therefore, the benefit of coaching for this one individual is:
>
> £114,000*0.5*1*0.95 = £54,150

However as explained above, the initial cost of the coaching is £5000. Therefore the actual net benefit is £49,150 which results in 9.83 ROI.

In this example, the coachee's behaviour change through coaching led to the organization realizing 9.83 times its investment in the coaching. Repeating this approach for the other five coachees gives a collated total for the individual ROI scores, but this won't tell you the benefit of the 'group' aspect of the coaching. In other words, how can you find out if the whole is greater than merely the sum of the parts? How did this group of people working together create a greater impact on the organization because they were coached together – how do you measure whether the whole is more than the sum of the parts? And this is partly the reason for exploring the wider system at the engagement stage, because there will be results that you are expecting that should come from the coaching process and there will be unintended results. In my business improvement role we used to play a game called 'whack a mole'. It's a very simple children's game where a mole appears and your task is to hit him over the head. You have no idea where he will next appear but the idea is to hit him as many times as possible. We used this in our workshops to illustrate the concept of variation. It is useful to reflect on this game in the context of ROI, since results achieved might just be the process working through normal variation; in other words, the system is creating the results.

Use the start and end points to create a journey

Getting to the heart of 'why?' is perhaps one of the most challenging up-front activities you do as a group coach. The group coaching process starts long before the first session and incorporates all stakeholders. I am often surprised at how little thought seemingly goes into this and how often organizations kick-start activities without doing a thorough assessment of the starting point or identifying what they expect to have changed by the end. Usually they will have thought about the numbers – for example, we want to increase profitability by x per cent or productivity by y per cent – without thoroughly understanding how they're realizing the current results. This base-lining activity is crucial if you are to really understand whether or not something is worth the effort, resources and energy to carry on. After all, if you don't know why you're doing something you can't measure it; you can only measure some of its characteristics like money or time. As we know, value equates to more than this. Ending without understanding the starting point suggests that you won't really know what the true value is.

KEY POINTS

- Results aren't produced in a vacuum – understanding the wider system at the start of a coaching relationship will help identify what to attribute to coaching and what is simply part of the wider system.

- Being clear about the reason why you're using group coaching rather than any other method lies at the heart of the measurement method you choose.

- Return on investment is only one measure – if you're using group coaching to liberate talent then return on growth and return on worth are less tangible but more meaningful long term measures.

- Be clear that ROI is not a pure science – it is subject to human interpretation and assessment, and can give a false sense of security simply because it is a number.

- Treat results as feedback and they will be more useful than if you treat them as finite fixed points – continuous learning and application of learning is the real result!

11

Measuring success in practice

The three core determinants of how your coachees perceive results: whether or not they've moved closer to their purpose, how well the contract created a safe and supportive environment and how they define success. If you've been coaching for a while, and particularly in the business environment, you'll be aware of the increasing focus on return on investment or the measurement of bottom line results from coaching. By now, it will be apparent that my take on this is somewhat different. The cause-and-effect philosophy that lies behind these perspectives provides a neat means of compartmentalizing action with results. In my experience of working with people, both one-to-one and in groups, I have found that rarely does A lead to B. It is more usual that A does something which then triggers C and so on, which leads to a result that impacts B. Where the key events occurred and who did what to create these results, and the degree of influence and impact they had, are difficult to measure. Having managed a large-scale improvement programme many years ago, I remember reflecting that although we had achieved great results, if I had been pushed to explain why, it would have been the result of many factors – not just one single thing. And even then, I would have had a low confidence rating for which factors had the most impact. And so this chapter moves into the more esoteric and less tangible measurement of success and wisdom.

You will probably have spotted by now that everything in this book can be used as a coaching tool with your group and here's another example: let's start with a simple exercise for you to do with a piece of paper and pen. Pick up the pen and start writing words that you associate with 'success'. Keep your mind free and allow the words to flow onto the page. When you've finished do the same activity but this time with 'wisdom'. Keep this paper to hand as you read through the chapter. You might want to ask your group to do this exercise as part of the contracting phase. You might even phrase it: 'Success or wisdom, what's important for you?'

Success is a matter of perspective

How many successful people have you coached? 'Successful' in this context means outwardly showing the signs of achievement and accomplishment. They might be highly qualified or have high-powered jobs or earn lots of money. For the average person, achieving the success of these people is something in their wildest dreams. So why is it that successful people seek coaching? It's all a matter of perspective – the outwardly seeming successful coachees perceive their attainments in a different way from the observer; what seems like success on the outside may be experienced as something very different on the inside.

In NLP there is a presupposition: there is no failure, only feedback. When measuring the 'success' of the coaching bear in mind this presupposition, particularly if you are using the group coaching process as a means of optimizing talents in your organization. 'Success' can sometimes be perceived as a single data point – achievement or failure. On the other hand, if 'success' is seen as movement towards your purpose then that changes your perspective significantly. It is useful to explore what lies behind the mindset of 'successful' people and the research of Dweck (2006), who observed that when children learn they seem not to be aware of the concept of 'failure' and, by virtue of that, 'success'. Each time they 'failed' they showed curiosity and excitement that they'd learnt something and had more new, cool things to learn. Their curiosity created a different label from the way we as adults perceive outcomes from our actions.

Starting with the end in mind means really being clear about what success means to your clients and coachees. How are they going to perceive success, and what's behind that? What have they learnt as they've journeyed through life that leads them to their definition? And where does success link back to their core purpose? Here's a simple exercise you can use, adapt, change or treat as a catalyst to create your own so that you can work with your group to discover what lies behind their definition of success.

Exercise

1   Give each coachee a piece of flipchart paper, some Post-it notes and a thick marker pen.

2   Ask them to draw a line that represents their life to date – they might draw a horizontal straight line, or a vertical straight line or a curvy line etc. Whatever makes sense and looks right to them.

3   Next, ask them to mark on that line the dates/times that they've experienced successes in their life so far and to write what that success was on a Post-it note and place it on their 'life line'.

4   When they've completed their 'success' diagram ask them to reflect what those successes were about.

5   When you've explored with them the meanings they attached to those successes, ask them to summarize on one Post-it note, in seven words or fewer, what lay behind those successes for them. What was the defining attribute or concept that caused those moments to be a success? If they can't 'chunk up' – ie work to the overriding concept behind that success – you could work through an exercise to elicit the highest level or theme. This exercise could be worked through in pairs.

6   Now that your coachees have identified their overriding theme for success, ask them to think about what success will look, feel and sound like for them once they have completed the coaching. Against their definition of success, how will they know that the coaching has been successful?

I'm guessing that there'll be a combination of different answers – some will be state changes: for example, the coachees will want to be more confident, assertive etc. And perhaps there will be some behavioural themes around learning new skills, such as presentation skills or interpersonal sensitivity; or there might be practical measures around having tools and techniques to deal with specific situations. Whatever their measures of success you will no doubt start to see patterns emerge as you work with different groups. The context will determine the specific themes that come out and there will be similarities across different groups – because we are all human and driven by similar needs, desires and motivations.

Returning to Dweck's research (2006), she posits that in Western societies in particular we measure our success by fixed points such as intelligence tests, exam results and so on. It is easy to understand how this happens. From the moment we are conceived we are measured against standards that have been set externally, for example weight and height indices. When we reach school age we are again subject to other standards such as reading levels, tests and so on. All through our life we start the learning process that in order to be 'successful' we have to measure against the standards set – by others. It is highly likely that your coachees and clients will be running the script that in order for the coaching to be successful, a standard of 'performance' has to be attained.

Have, do or be: which measure does your group use?

Thinking about this fixed-point approach to success, look at your group's list of definitions of success – where do they lie on the 'have, do or be' continuum? Here's another simple exercise that you might wish to use or adapt to find out more about the coachees' definitions of success. To help with the exercise, in this context 'have' = material objects, 'do' = activities and attainments, and 'be' = inner states.

Exercise

For this exercise you will need three hula hoops (or more if you are going to ask the coachees to do this individually: ie three hula hoops per coachee). You can buy them from most children's toy stores. The brighter the colour the better!

1 Take the hula hoops and place them on the floor as in Figure 11.1.

2 Ask the coachees to place their Post-it notes upon which they've written the times in their life when they've been successful into the relevant hoop. For example, if they've passed a degree that would be a 'do', having their dream car would be a 'have' and so on.

3 There might be some overlap between the categories and it is up to the coachees how much they feel this overlap is – hence using hula hoops because you can change the size of the overlap. Equally there might be no overlap and the hula hoops are completely separate.

4 Walk round the room to review how they're categorizing their 'successes' – sometimes a 'be' is in fact a 'do' or 'have'.

5 Allow as much time as the group needs. This is a reflective exercise and is designed to get the coachees to challenge their own ideas about where their successes lie.

6 Once they've completed this activity, carry out a review and ask them for their thoughts feelings and insights from what they've done and now see.

FIGURE 11.1

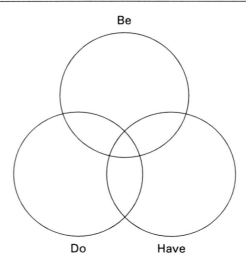

Encourage discussion, reflection and deep thought around this exercise, and handle it with care. Sometimes the very act of 'seeing' what we carry in our mind and gaining insights about what that might be about can be very powerful and sometimes evoke emotional responses. Constantly take the 'temperature' of the room by sensing the energy and emotion and possible resistance, and be ready to support and work through with the coachees on anything as it comes up. There are no right or wrong answers to this exercise; it is simply a means of exploring what lies behind the definitions of success that the coachees live with daily and how this might be influencing their views of what they're really learning. They might be discounting 'successes' or including activities that, on reflection, aren't 'successes' at all. It is all about their perspective and understanding where they place importance and meaning – have, do or be.

You will now have worked with them on their definitions of success and the criteria they use, which will hopefully help them formulate what their coaching journey is about and how they will be monitoring progress rather than just measuring success.

Wisdom is self-perpetuating

Earlier in our coaching journey we explored the choice of approaching group coaching as a tick-box activity or as a process – the choice is down to you as the coach and the nature of the topics on which you are coaching. The notion of coaching as a process, or journey, means there is opportunity for continuous growth and learning, and for me this is where the true 'success' of coaching lies. Narrow definitions of success suggest attainment or achievement of some 'thing' – that is, an externally referenced thing. From my own experience of being coached, the benefits are more about the intrinsic stuff. The 'intrinsic stuff' is the learning and insights that project from the coaching experience and remain with you as you continue to learn and grow. Talent development is about harnessing the intrinsic motivation and, through application and determination, creating perpetual growth. Looking back at the children in Dweck's research, just imagine what could be possible if we were to retain that child-like curiosity and freedom from labels such as success and failure. What might we achieve if we were to live in that world? We usually ask our clients and coachees to think about how they will measure success; maybe we should ask them instead to think about how they will increase their wisdom through the process.

You can view coaching as something that brings about transactional changes: for example, coachees who want to improve how they present – the mechanics of how they're preparing, what their vision and script of a successful presentation is, what their options are in order to improve and so on. Or you can view coaching as something that brings about transformational change – in other words, something shifts at a deeper level that permanently changes the perspective of the coachee and opens up new worlds for them to explore. At this level of change you are coaching them around their beliefs and values and working with them on the assumptions that are maybe getting in their way. They start to live the presupposition that there is no failure, only feedback, and glimmers of that child-like curiosity come to the surface. In this view of coaching, success points become mere markers in their journey; in other words they are feedback mechanisms that provide results that feed into a systemic view of progress and purpose. The success points are not end points; they are jumping-off points for further growth. Transformational coaching fosters humility within the coachee that there will be times when the results aren't favourable – but these too are merely jumping-off points for further learning. The wisdom comes from recognizing the wider system in which the results are being experienced so that the coachee doesn't just lurch from action to action without truly reflecting and seeking understanding as to what might be happening to create those results.

The other shift I think is when they start to take their new-found way of interacting outside of their groups into another, other groups inside the org, outside the organization. Those are probably the most exciting times in coaching... As a coach I feel proud – Yes! There's something really in this, it works. You can see it's actually making a difference to the whole organization. So I think the best experiences are when you're able to facilitate that kind of difference and it's actually really starting to have a whole system effect not just group specifically. In today's world, I believe the stakes are high for what coaches must help enable – there is so much at risk in the world and so much resource available in the world to assist that risk, but people need help changing their mental models, and group coaching is how this can be enabled. So, if you're having a good experience within the team that's not really enough anymore; I believe the call for coaches and coachees today is to enable that impact to spread beyond the first team of focus, to spread the learning... People naturally tend to play small or feel that whole system change is too overwhelming for them to take on. With more great examples of group coaching, this will change in time.

Lorna McDowell, Xenergie

The challenge with taking a 'success' measurement only is that the coachee treats each effect as if it were caused by their action, when in fact it might not have been. Looking back at my own example earlier – I honestly cannot say what actions caused the 'success' with the programme I managed. All I can say is that the results were favourable. A wisdom-based approach to measurement applies humility and recognition that sometimes the system creates 'luck' and the egocentric nature of 'success'-based measurements claim cause-and-effect links that in reality don't exist.

When you ask your coachees the question 'What are you looking to find from the coaching – success or wisdom?' – explore with them which of the two will serve them in the long term. Success is transitory and contextually driven whereas wisdom by its very nature self-perpetuates. Knowing which questions to ask and having the humility to acknowledge when you don't know something are both great opportunities for learning and growth. Perhaps the reason measurement of coaching creates such debate is because of another facet of our humanity: the need for recognition.

Peter Senge's seminal book (1990, 2006 edition) changed the nature of how we view learning within organizations. As part of the research for this book I revisited *The Fifth Discipline* and having decided to read the Introduction was surprised to read that Senge had asked W Edwards Deming to write the foreword to the 1990 edition. My introduction to group coaching started when I moved into a business improvement role, and a great deal of that learning was an introduction to the System of Profound Knowledge by Deming – to whom I now realize I owe a great deal for my own philosophies about working with people and culture.

Recognition

At the beginning of our journey together we explored some of the concepts within transactional analysis (TA) – Eric Berne's theory of human behaviour and personality. One of the theories he expounded was that needs drive human behaviours, which Berne called hungers. These are important to understand in relation to how your coachees and you define success and what your perspective is on the need for recognition. The drivers behind our need for success, and hence recognition, are telling features of how we're likely to measure that success and what that means about how we see ourselves in relation to others. I don't intend to provide a deep analysis of TA here, merely to offer my approach on how to use this knowledge (and hopefully wisdom) to help coach others. Part of the concept of egoless coaching derives from this concept within TA and may serve you as a coach or at least create some food for thought.

This is how I describe the two basic needs:

- The need for connection – knowing that you are not alone, the physical and psychological connections that you create and feel with others.

- The need for recognition – that you count and your existence makes a difference.

Berne describes the way these evolve as starting with the hunger for human contact when we are babies, which then through a process of metamorphosis becomes the need for recognition in the form of 'strokes' – these can either be conditional or unconditional. The conditional positive stroke is usually a recognition based around achievement or recognition: eg 'good girl/boy you did really well in your exams.' The unconditional stroke is based on just being you: eg 'you're a wonderful human being.' It is likely that we will all have experienced more of the conditional strokes than the unconditional strokes. We will probably all have experienced some of the negative strokes that associate what we've done with who we are: eg 'you're useless for failing that exam.' Berne called this the 'stroke economy' in that we are all striving to gain more and more positive strokes and our strategies for achieving this soon become apparent based on the experiences we've had during our formative childhood years. As we discussed at the beginning of this book, coaching is not therapy but sometimes it can be therapeutic, and sometimes we use tools from other fields to help us. Without getting too wrapped up in analysing why a coachee might be running with different strategies to achieve recognition through 'success', let's explore some simple exercises that might draw out what lies deeper behind their perspective on success and how they can use anything that comes out from the coaching in a positive way that will maintain their self-esteem and create a safe haven for positive unconditional regard.

Wisdom around human behaviours suggest that we are always successful if we view it that way because human beings are perfectly flawed; if we weren't we would never have the capacity to grow or develop. Here's a simple exercise I was shown by one of the delegates on a workshop and that I've used many times since. It's a visual representation of what I've just described.

Exercise

1 Take a £10 note (or one of similar value in another currency) and ask the group 'How much is it worth?'

2 Next, crumple up the £10 note and ask them again 'How much is this worth?'

Hopefully the group will say that the note is still worth the same. The creases and folds on the £10 note represent the situations when things don't go so well, and maybe these represent failures. Ask the group how much they will be worth if they don't achieve the measures they've set themselves for the coaching. This will no doubt create an interesting discussion and there will be possible resistance based on how they've received recognition in the past. This is one of those occasions where sometimes information on the process can help the group. Ask the group if they would like more content and if so, explain a little more about how the concept works. Once you've done this, ask them what came to mind for them as you were explaining this. Allow moments of silence for the group to process what they're discovering. Sometimes, just allowing the silence and then moving on creates the space for the group to internalize what their success really is about for them. You could, if you wish, ask them to do some 'homework' and write a reflective piece or journal about what's come up for them as a result of the session. Even if nothing has come up, that in itself is interesting.

Here's another exercise you could you use to explore this notion of recognition and worth – the fact that sometimes we look for external measures of worth when the reality is we are already worthy as human beings.

Exercise

1   Invite your coachees to take a piece of paper – at least A4 size.

2   Divide the paper into two columns vertically and invite your coachees to write down in the right-hand column all the things they want to do, be or have.

3   When they have done this, ask them to score each item on a scale of 1–10 where 10 is high, where they are in relation to that item.

4   In the left-hand column invite them to write down everything that makes them a wonderful human being.

5   When they've finished ask them to label the right-hand column 'doing' and the left hand-column 'being'.

6   Invite them to spend a few minutes reflecting on what they've written and comparing the lists.

7   When the time feels right, open up a discussion asking questions to allow their learning, eg what do they notice?

I usually invite the coachees to imagine what would happen if there were an impenetrable wall between the two lists – the being side could never, ever go below 10 because as human beings we are always OK and the 'doing' side is open to change as we learn and develop new skills, abilities and talents. This usually creates interesting discussions, and as a final question I ask what insights have come up for them and how they will use what they have realized in developing their success and 'failure' strategy for the coaching.

Our need for recognition creates our strategy for success, and if that recognition is based on conditional positive strokes our failure strategy is going to feel pretty tough. It is far better to create a success strategy that is balanced with a failure strategy; one based on investment in a child-like curiosity so that we and our coachees view failure as an opportunity to learn. Better still, delete the words success and failure from your vocabulary and insert the words learning and growth. Success by its nature is egocentric and cries out for adulation from others at what we have achieved. The true purpose of coaching is to develop our inherent need to learn and grow free from the constraints of externally set standards that we absorb without conscious thought. Egoless coaching is recognizing that there will be days when the external view of success will not be our own internal view of progress towards our purpose. Fixed-point success measures are great ways to create conditional positive strokes but not so great at giving true recognition.

Success and wisdom in the real world

I started this chapter by coming clean with you that my views on success and measurement are different from the accepted ways of defining success in business. In the real world the clients and/or coachees want to know that they've got benefit from the coaching experience. That is the reality you as group coaches will be familiar with, and you will also want to know that the interventions you've used have provided some value to your clients. What I offer to you here is a different way of measuring that benefit. The ultimate measure of group coaching is whether the coachees themselves have moved forward in reaching their purpose and, if you're working in an organizational setting, whether the coaching has helped the organization move forward as well. If they have then the coaching has achieved its purpose. Hopefully having read this you will have another perspective on fixed-point success measures and start to see that talent development is a journey that continues forever. Measuring one point on that continuum is merely feedback on progress and, whilst it may recognize something as a great result, it is not success in the true sense. Success is about moving forward, and sometimes to move forward you need to step back. There is no failure only feedback – it's all about mindset and perspective.

KEY POINTS

- 'Success' is a matter of perspective and when seen as movement on a continuum towards your purpose creates a growth and learning mindset.
- Recognition, success and worth are integrally linked – help your coachees explore how they define and ascribe meaning to each.
- Success is a 'fixed-point' mindset – the real question is, has the group coaching been beneficial and worthwhile?
- Balancing success with failure is important, and helping your coachees develop a healthy failure strategy based on child-like curiosity is the real trick to measuring success.

PART FIVE
Group coaching as talent liberation

Using group coaching as part of your talent system

12

L et me take you back to the very beginning of this book and pose the question about your purpose for group coaching. What is the reason that you are interested in group coaching and in particular the reason why optimizing collective talent is important to you? If you want to use group coaching as part of your talent system then there are number of important factors you will need to consider:

- The purpose behind using group coaching as part of your talent system.
- They reason why that's important.
- What the likely benefits might be.
- Diagnosing your current talent system and getting clear on your talent strategy.
- Group coaching creates a learning organization system – there are benefits and consequences to this.
- Is group coaching the only tool in your box to achieve your purpose?

The purpose behind group coaching as part of your talent system

In Chapter 1 we explored what our purpose is and that it has to be something more than just an objective. It's a combination of legacy and something higher than us. Here I share Lorna McDowell's explanation of what this means to her within an organization:

My discovery of group coaching started with a question – how do you actually get the human dynamics in an organization to work really well so that the inside and the outside are coherent, and that communications actually come together much more synergistically so that there isn't so much wastage?

In drafting out your purpose for using group coaching to optimize collective talents, dig deep into what it means for your organization. How will the organization be different, and in what way? What's the best scenario that might come out of this for your organization? Maybe look back at some of the tools from Part 3 to find a tool that could help you explore the purpose for you and your organization. The next question becomes why: why is that important to you?

The reason why that's important

Back in Chapter 2 we talked about the benefits from group coaching and the underlying reasons behind benefits – the fact that the overt payoffs might mask the true reasons why they are important. I'm guessing that if you're interested in exploring how you might use group coaching in your organization you've already got some solid reasons why it's important for you. I am also fully versed in the 'latest fad' reason, which is usually presented in a politically correct way – but I've explained how this reason is likely to fall at the first hurdle because it hasn't been thought through in depth. Here are eight reasons that I've outlined throughout this book that I've summarized and that might be relevant for you. If your reasons are different, that's great; I am not attempting to mind-read, merely offer some ideas to catalyse your thinking.

- Organizations are comprised of individual human beings. We are most productive when we harness our resources and talents collectively.

- Group dynamics in an organizational setting become the system. Group coaching gives direct experience of how to work in the system since it becomes a sub-system of the whole.

- Group coaching provides opportunities to develop networks across the organization and the tools to do this long after the coaching finishes.

- The talent system encompasses the whole organization – it's about how you attract, reward, develop, engage and retain people. Group coaching helps ignite enthusiasm and interest in creating solutions and increases levels of engagement.

- Group coaching when integrated with the talent system provides a sustainable model for continuous improvement – from both a personal development and an organizational development perspective.

- When people are coached together in groups it counters some of the systems constraints that can occur (particularly in autocratic, hierarchical systems) and aids organizational change.

- Group coaching brings people from all disciplines and functions together in a way that is not usual – this is a catalyst for breaking down some of the silos that might be present in the organization.

- Group coaching gives permission for people to reflect and think together – to share joint responsibility for supporting and helping each other, which encourages collaborative thinking and provides an environment to experience constructive conflict. This in turn enables difficult conversations within the organization.

What other reasons did you come up with? There are no right or wrong answers since the reasons will probably be dictated by the context that has brought you to consider group coaching as a means of optimizing collective talents. Ultimately, understanding the reasons why it's important links back to your overriding purpose. That purpose has to inspire you to take action and commit to bringing energy to see it through to conclusion. Part of that action will be to explore thoroughly and thoughtfully the 'reason why' and 'so that', which were discussed in the part on measurement. Clarity on how group coaching will help you improve or maintain your talent system creates the energy for action, so let's explore some of the benefits that you might expect.

What the likely benefits might be

Your talent system encompasses the way people are attracted to the organization, how they're motivated when they're at work, what level of engagement they have in their daily activities and how much of their potential has been developed. Group coaching therefore has to be applied in ways that directly address the key challenges within your talent system. These challenges are likely to come from your purpose and reasons 'why' above. I've listed four major benefits that may or may not be on your list:

- Problems get resolved faster because people know how to work together productively and have tools for generating solutions.
- Productivity potentially increases because people are more engaged in what they do.
- The organization creates more flow in that challenging tasks are matched to skill and talents, meaning that people are able to tackle more challenging work – this also has a knock-on effect to attraction, engagement and retention levels.
- The organizational system evolves and works in a more conscious way – the people within the system are able to apply intelligent choices to tough dilemmas.

The organization starts to generate improved results across a whole range of indices through these benefits, and the system generates a positive feedback loop.

It should be pointed out that to attain these benefits takes time and continuous work – systems change slowly (where they do change) so the ultimate benefit is that group coaching, when incorporated with your talent system, creates organizational learning and continuous improvement. And this leads to the next consideration, which is diagnosing your current talent system.

Diagnosing your current talent system

Throughout this book I have discussed the importance of understanding the system and being aware that the system is unpredictable. The generic talent system – attraction, reward, development, engagement and retention – will be present in all organizations that employ people. How systems work in practice will be very different even if on the surface they look the same. Here's my earlier definition of 'system': 'a collection of interconnected processes, mechanisms, beliefs, actions, behaviours and assumptions grouped and defined by the context in which they operate' (Chapter 10).

For example, the processes might be similar but the experience within the organization will be different. And the reason is the culture; the culture creates the system. Before you use group coaching or any intervention, it is extremely helpful to reflect and map out what you believe the system is like in reality. That is, how you experience the system in practice. For example, how do people really get promoted in your organization? What are the values that really matter when push comes to shove? The reason it's important to have at least a basic understanding of the system before you introduce group coaching is that you need to have some idea of the likely consequences of adding that ingredient into the mix. What do you think might be the consequences and where might there be ripples within the system? Systems by their nature are complex beasts, and it will be challenging to have 100 per cent certainty about your talent system. The key here is to have just enough understanding to be able to surmise what might happen.

The talent system is a holistic view of how people experience the organization, and talent management is the practical way in which that system is operated day to day. In purist terms, talent management is the responsibility of all managers and leaders within the organization. The reality is sometimes that the HR function carries out the talent management activities – in other words, we return to our old friend the 'tick list' – talent management is seen as an activity rather than a process. Using group coaching to optimize collective talents will return the benefits we discussed earlier when it is introduced in a holistic way not in a piecemeal, tick-list way. The basic coaching system that lies behind any coaching model incorporates continuous improvement – when you coach people in groups you are coaching them to learn both continuous improvement and systems based thinking. Having that experience of learning together multiplies the learning effect because you are able to use other's learning to catalyse your own insights.

If you are going to use group coaching as part of your talent system, then understanding the upsides and downsides of that system is crucial before taking any action. I talk about 'Pandora's Box' in one of my tools; if you embark on coaching people in groups without thinking it through, at best you will disengage people as they might feel it is 'just another initiative' and at worst frustrate them because the 'system' creates barriers to implementing what they learn during the coaching. All the negative energy will dissipate throughout the coaching groups and cynicism is sure to follow. Once you've created a basic model of the talent system – and the trick here is to capture just enough to help you decide what to do and where – the next thing to consider is your talent strategy. We talked earlier about your group coaching strategy, and if you are using group coaching in an organization then the two activities run hand in hand. Working with the group coach you will obtain more benefits from the group coaching process if you dovetail your strategies and discuss openly and honestly any potential areas of difficulty or barriers.

Getting clear on your talent strategy

First of all, let me remind you of my definition of strategy from Chapter 4: 'A strategy is an overarching, decisive course of action that will lead you to your objective.'

Your strategy tells you where you going to commit resources, time and energy to a course of action in preference to any other course of action. In talent management terms there are two strategies: inclusive or exclusive.

Exclusive talent strategy

There is a prevailing topic in discussions relating to talent that is known as the 'war for talent', or as I prefer to call it the scarcity talent principle. This assumes that talent is a limited resource, that it is a fixed commodity held only by the few. A model that might be familiar to you is the nine-box model (Figure 12.1), which in its basic form sets out to chart potential against performance. This is the favoured model for mapping talent within organizations and is an elongated version of the proverbial four-box model made popular by most consultants – and I include myself in that grouping! Taken at face value this model is a useful way, particularly in large multi-site organizations, of taking a snapshot of what is happening with the people who work in the organization. It shows at a glance where there are performance dips and potential left untapped. The operative word in that sentence is 'snapshot'. The model is intended to be a statement at one point in time. What typically tends to happen is that labels are assigned to the different boxes, and I've illustrated this (Figure 12.2) to demonstrate the kind of labels used in these boxes. Organizations tend to use their own language to describe the 'categories' of people within those boxes but this diagram gives you an idea of the labels that become associated with those 'boxes' and, inadvertently, the people become labelled by virtue of being placed in those boxes. The next logical step for this type of approach is to identify who forms the 'talent pool' within the organization (Figure 12.3). I have circled the most likely talent pool definition, although some organizations might well include one or maybe two of the adjoining boxes – depending on the size of the organization. This approach is what I call an exclusive talent management strategy because it assumes that the people outside that 'magic ring' do not qualify as 'talent' in the way that the organization sees it. In fact, the boxes to the left-hand lower corner are assumed to have no potential or low potential.

FIGURE 12.1

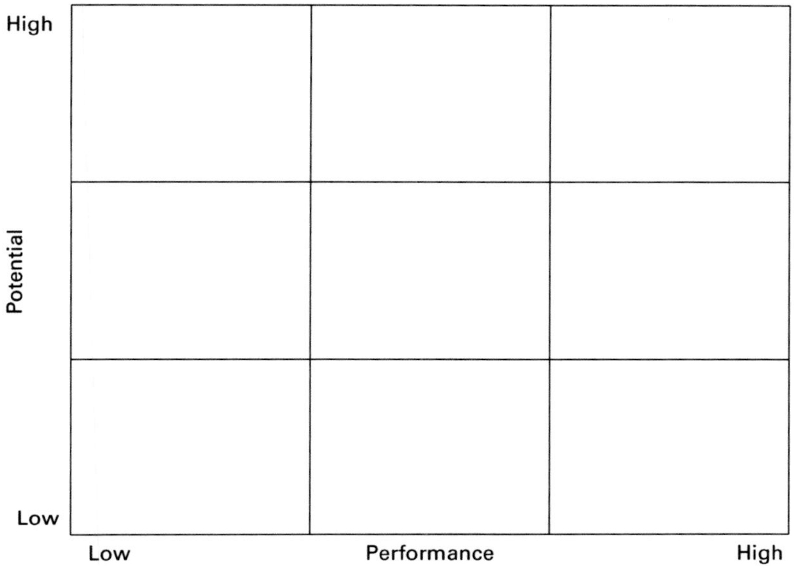
High
Potential
Low
Low
Performance
High

FIGURE 12.2

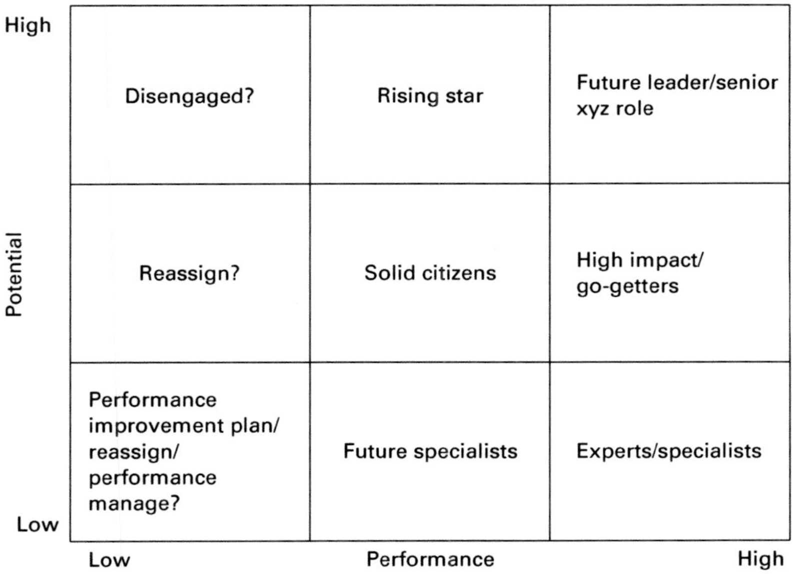
High
Potential
Low
Disengaged?
Rising star
Future leader/senior xyz role
Reassign?
Solid citizens
High impact/ go-getters
Performance improvement plan/ reassign/ performance manage?
Future specialists
Experts/specialists
Low
Performance
High

FIGURE 12.3

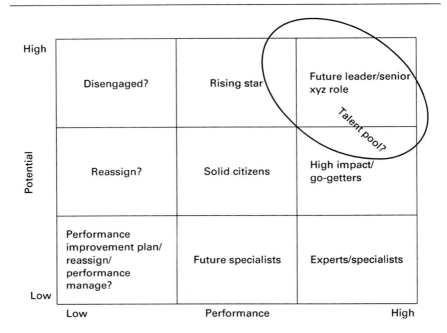

If your talent system is based on an exclusive talent strategy this will mean the scope of the coaching is likely to apply to those falling within the 'top talent' pool. Be aware that this approach has consequences for the way group coaching is likely to be perceived. The coaching – because it is a scarce commodity – is likely to stimulate demand from those outside the 'talent pool'. How you manage that demand requires careful consideration. You will also need to consider how this approach might impact your wider engagement and retention strategy. Disenchanted employees outside the 'talent pool' who feel snubbed because they don't have access to the coaching might actively start to disengage or look for alternative work. How much attrition from outside your 'talent pool' can the organization carry? What level of disengagement is likely to impact productivity and what indices are likely to tell you this? There is also the 'prima donna' syndrome that some-times comes from labelling employees 'top talent'. Therefore the effects of your strategy on the wider system need to be considered and options identi-fied as to how they can be offset.

FIGURE 12.4

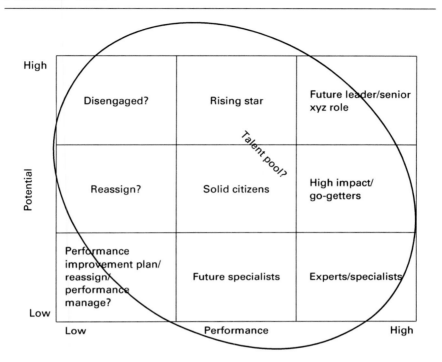

Inclusive strategy

This strategy sees group coaching as a tool to optimize performance and liberate the talents of everyone. So the talent pool will be the whole organization (Figure 12.4). An inclusive strategy on talent asserts that if you take a simple definition of coaching as 'helping people improve', then helping them find hidden talents and putting energy into developing those talents must be equally beneficial for those who are already demonstrating high performance levels as for those who are not. In fact, you could argue that helping those who are performing less well work out what's holding them back – and it could be the organizational system they're working in – could help the organization become even more productive. In continuous improvement terms you are raising the performance level of the whole organization through coaching everyone, not just the selected few. The upside to this strategy is that it opens up possibilities for creating an environment for skills development and job movement within the organization that helps it grow organically without falling back on the external market. In effect, this creates an internal micro-economy within the organization. The downside is that it takes concentrated time and effort to apply this strategy to everyone and it can seem untargeted.

The perspective the client holds will have implications for the content of the group coaching and the context. The organization systems and culture and the prevailing talent culture and strategy will impact both the mechanism and membership of groups to be coached. There are challenges for the coach in both perspectives. Which of these strategies reflects your organization? Do you wish to change your strategy and are you using group coaching to help do that? If so, it is even more important that you have a big picture view of your talent system and understand where there might be areas of resistance. And this leads us to the final area of consideration if you wish to use group coaching as part of your talent system. We have alluded to it already but it's important to recognize that this can be a show-stopper for some organizations. This final area is group coaching as a mechanism to create a learning organization.

Group coaching creates a learning organization system

Most organizations know that creating an organizational learning system is logically a good thing to do; very few either understand what that really means or, if they do, want to experience the reality. Group coaching at its heart creates a learning system – coachees experience the coaching process and learn how to learn. Otherwise, what's the point of the coaching? Your role as coach is in effect to become redundant in the process as the coachee learns how to self-coach. Coaching people together in groups means they have an opportunity to experiment with and explore how to interact in a positive learning environment with others. They practise the learning system inside the coaching sessions and, although the topic will be different each time, the learning system will be the same. If you use group coaching systematically and organization-wide there is a point at which the sheer volume of numbers creates a shift and the learning behaviours experienced in the coaching sessions will become the behaviours demonstrated outside the coaching as well. In creating a system for learning you open up the possibility that people in the organization will start to ask sometimes challenging questions, and that they will expect to be able to come up with creative solutions and take responsibility for their actions. That is what the coaching process teaches them.

The question therefore remains whether this is the sort of learning system you want to create. How far along the continuum do you wish to go? How much time, energy and resource are you willing to put in to create a true learning organization? It could be that your culture and system is not yet ready for this level of challenge. Keeping your focus on the purpose and reasons why you're embarking on the group coaching journey means that you can flex your strategy to suit the context. And there may be other means of helping optimize collective talents that are less 'disruptive' in the sense of upsetting the equilibrium. One-to-one coaching is certainly a great means of optimizing individual talents but it falls short of leveraging the benefit of bringing people together to learn how to learn collectively.

Is group coaching the only tool in your box to achieve your purpose?

You will no doubt have many different tools in your talent development box, and by now will have come to a conclusion about whether group coaching is something you wish to pursue as part of your talent system. The value of group coaching is that it is designed to provide an experience of working in a system – ie the group – that other methods such as one-to-one coaching aren't. The learning experience of group coaching within organizations is as much about how the individuals interact with each other as it is about their coaching topic. One of the key aims of coaching people together is to equip them with the tools to navigate interpersonal relationships – particularly in organizations. Group dynamics are a sub-set of the system dynamics and the group coaching environment provides a relatively risk-free environment for coachees to reflect and explore the behavioural factors at play within the wider system. These are the 'click-whirr' responses that often occur simply because people behave in accordance with the system. Coachees learn skills through experiencing the coaching process that they can apply directly to how they behave within the organization and make intelligent choices about everyday dilemmas. They learn how to learn. The nature of group work means that they already start to apply that systems learning within the coaching sessions.

Group coaching can be done as a one-off activity not linked to anything else – this is the 'tick-list' approach we discussed in Chapter 4. Or it can be integrated with the talent system so that it becomes the way to help talent flourish. Using group coaching as part of your talent system has to be done in a planned and thoughtful way with full appreciation of consequences –

intended or not – that are likely to ensue from coaching people how to think and challenge the status quo. In the next chapter I share some thoughts on actions you might wish to consider if you decide that group coaching is something you want to incorporate in your talent system.

KEY POINTS

- Using group coaching as part of your talent system has to serve a higher purpose to elevate it from an activity.

- Really clarify the value that the talent system will gain from group coaching and be clear about the consequences, positive or negative, that might ensue.

- Understand your talent strategy before you embark on group coaching so that you can work with your coach/es to integrate your approach.

- Acknowledge both the upsides and downsides of your current talent strategy and be mindful of the wider system if you are seeking to use group coaching as the means to change it.

- Be honest about how comfortable your organization is with employees really using their brains – do you really want people to learn?

Actions for optimizing collective talent

13

Group coaching is about harnessing the collective talent of individuals who come together for the purpose of learning and development. And there's something special about that collaboration, about being together with other human beings and expressing our inherent need to be social, to work with other people, to learn with other people. As we reach the final chapter in the book I want to bring out the purpose of the book: that optimizing and leveraging the grouping of people brings benefits that no other form of personal development methods will achieve – because other methods focus on the individual and, as we know, we live in social systems. The focus of group coaching is learning and developing together in a group to create a social system for that learning, and that's the whole point really. Performing both singing and acting gives a great buzz and you can feel the adrenalin start to pump, but there's something special about performing with other people, particularly singing. Group singing gives a resonance in your chest, and when you reach the notes together you can feel that group energy, that group talent, coming together. It's the same effect you experience with group coaching, that metaphorical resonance of 'performing' at your best. And that's what group coaching is about. It's about experiencing something that is greater than us, and for me that's why it is about purpose: it's about achieving or realizing something that is greater than we would have achieved or realized on our own. Of course individual coaching brings out talents; it brings out individuals' inherent capabilities that they didn't even know they had. The beauty of working in a group and coaching people in groups is that they get an opportunity to experience and observe how other people experience talents developing, and having that experience they realize that they can be more than they are. Experiencing and observing that in others provides a brilliant opportunity to for us to create insights about our own capabilities and what we might be doing that's getting in the way of reaching and manifesting those capabilities.

The whole purpose of this book is about finding ways of generating positive and productive collaborative working, and in this last chapter I remind you of the key points from each of the other chapters and give you some final thoughts and ideas about how you can do this because I would like to you to commit to taking action. I would like you to think about what you can do in your group coaching that will build on and generate that moment when people truly experience the progress of others and maybe see things in others that they don't see in themselves. Because somehow the ability to spot, observe and pinpoint someone else's talent helps you understand through coaching that there may be talents you are missing about yourself. As you look through the key points from each of the chapters, think about what you are doing now in your group coaching, in your organization that will enhance that collaborative spirit, and what you could do in addition or differently to manifest your purpose. The sense that the whole is more than just the sum of the parts means that coaching people in groups is not just additive or incremental, it's an exponential experience.

Creating momentum by going back to basics

One of the tools I offer as an idea to move you to action is around a concept that is really built on the true home of coaching – Socratic dialogue. The concept is the 'world cafe' and some of you may already be familiar with it. I am grateful to my colleagues at the Talent Management Association in the UK who used this at one of their conferences I attended as it was a brilliant experience for me and reminded me why all great coaching starts and ends with great questions. The exercise using this concept brought out the collective wisdom of the group and a few months later by sheer chance a client asked me to work with their team using the concept of the world cafe. I had an opportunity to put into practice what I'd learnt and the client was willing to experiment with the concept – the groundwork was already laid because child-like curiosity is a prerequisite for this method. Having been a participant and a facilitator of the process, I learnt different things about how that basic principle of Socratic dialogue and Socratic questioning brings out the inherent wisdom we all have and that, if we truly listen, we build on when we talk with others.

So what is the world cafe? It's based on the concept of conversations you have over coffee with your friends in the local cafe. The principle being that when you go into a cafe environment you're likely to be more relaxed and the creative side of your thinking is more likely to be switched on. The first part of creating a world cafe is that the setting is all-important. It has to have that cafe environment feel to evoke relaxation and freedom from a work environment or an environment where you're thinking through a problem. It's about taking that problem out of it, relaxing and simply being present in the moment. So the first aspect is the environment and making you feel really present and truly connected in the moment. To create this environment it is even better if you can 'hire' a cafe or create a 'mock' cafe in a room – this means finding appropriate tables and chairs, having drinks available, cakes – anything that creates a representation of a cafe setting. It is also worth having paper tablecloths and chunky pens so that people can doodle or write ideas and thoughts as they come up. The groups usually find their own way of working with this.

The second part behind the concept is that you ask challenging questions, and this is where you are looking to tap into people's inherent capability by asking them to think deeply about the questions. The questions have to be phrased in a way that is very open and allows for discussion. 'What' is a key word in the questions? Even a challenging statement that gets people to discuss. The more challenging the better, because what you want is to tap into the reason why it's important for people. So this second part is that the questions have to be phrased in a way that generates purposeful enquiry and avoids 'critical thinking' or problem-solving type discussions. There are no right or wrong answers to the questions and the more philosophical the better.

The next part in setting up the world cafe is about the nature of the group – world cafe is designed for groups really of greater than eight people upwards. It can work really well with big groups; in the first experience I had there were about 100 people in the room and in the second there were around 50. The bigger the group the better because what you're really doing is tapping into the collective whole and collecting and synthesizing as many different views as possible. The cafe environment means that you have tables with around six to eight chairs at each table. The smallest number of people at each table ideally is six, and part of the fun of this method is that you can work with it, adapt it and reflect on what works better for your groups. Keeping the groups to a maximum of eight people works better because it gives everyone a chance to talk and think, particularly those with an introvert preference. The idea is that you want to create an environment in which everybody has an opportunity to talk and share together with everyone through the use of smaller groups.

The fact that everyone has the opportunity to share even in larger groups is achieved through physical movement around the room. Groups will be given a specific amount of time to discuss the questions and topics before being asked to move onto different tables. They can choose which table they join, with the overriding principle that the tables should have a maximum and minimum number of participants. To ensure that there is linkage and connection between the different conversations there is a facilitator at each table, and this is where you can introduce the coaching element because this is an ideal way of using group coaching in an informal way in an organization that makes it accessible for all. Each table has a coach who will be working possibly more in facilitator mode but using inherent coaching skills to bring out the conversations and to ensure everyone has the opportunity to be involved in the conversation and keep the conversation flowing – or not. You purposely might want to create moments of silence for people to reflect and think about what they've heard. I noticed this happened naturally with some groups anyway. The idea is that the coach/facilitator is the anchor point for the conversation, because as people move between tables the coach/facilitator will stay behind and as people join the table will recap what happened from the previous conversations and ask the new members joining the table to recap what came up at their tables. So the idea is that you create movement around the tables as a physical manifestation of the conversation moving on – it's a very physical tool. It's the idea of building on ideas and conversations and exploring new ways of seeing and thinking about them.

There are a few ground rules and I've mentioned some of them already, but that's the basic principle of how the world cafe works. I've outlined the key points of the process. It is up to you and the groups how you work it in practice – experiment and develop ways to make this work for you. There is a great online resource from which you can print out materials and find out more about the ethos behind the 'world cafe' and this can be found in the reference section of the book.

Basic concept

- Opportunity to explore some questions informally – the number of questions will be determined by the amount of time available.
- Move round the tables.
- Thinking as well as talking.
- Enjoy the process whilst having a cup of coffee (or tea!)

Basic ground rules

- There are no 'right answers'.
- Play with the questions – enjoy the conversations.
- Take a different perspective from normal – see what happens.
- Get curious.
- Tables of six to eight people.
- Discuss the question and add to it.
- Keep conversations free from judgement – get curious.
- Thinking not solution!

Practical considerations

- The participants can make notes and draw on the paper tablecloths – these can be collected and used to work out what you will do with the collective wisdom in the room.
- Use a bell or something audible to let people know when it's time to move on to the next table – making this a funny sound creates humour and adds to the relaxed feeling.
- Coach/facilitator stays behind to summarize for the next people joining the table.
- Allow at least 10 minutes for each 'table' conversation before moving people on. A maximum of three rounds for the same question and a maximum of three different questions in total seems to be the limit. Allow plenty of time for the whole session.
- Consider whether you want a 'coffee break' between each different question for people to replenish their coffee cups and take comfort breaks. Judge this by the energy in the room.

Whether or not you're using group coaching in your organization or coaching practice, this is a great way to bring clients together. If you're working in a coaching practice, this is a method of bringing all of your individual clients together so that they can tap into each other's collective wisdom. Clearly you will need to ensure that your clients are willing to participate, and you might want to have some agreement as to how this will work in practice; after all it's a great opportunity for them to learn from others even if there might not be any immediate synergies. And in an organization setting, you need to be prepared for some of the conversations that will come out of this, and also be prepared for what you're going to do with what comes out of those conversations. How are you going to use the energy created by those conversations to give people a sense of flow and engagement in their day-to-day jobs? What is the 'system' in which you are looking to leverage collective talent. What foundation and basis have you got in place around the leveraging of collective talent? Do you have something in place? Is it something that you want you to develop? Perhaps the world cafe concept could be a means of developing or creating systemic change in your organization. There are at least three benefits from the world cafe concept:

- It leverages collective wisdom and brings out energy around that wisdom.
- If it's done purposefully and systematically it has the opportunity to cause systemic change. Essentially, whether you're looking at the individual or you're looking at the group, coaching is about creating systemic change.
- It engages people in meaningful dialogue and starts to create the means for collaborative working.

Optimizing talent is really continuous improvement – it's about tapping into the inherent capabilities we all have and understanding how you're going to use those talents to improve things either incrementally or for revolutionizing systemic change.

Leveraging the group to optimize their talents

Talent requires three basic ingredients to flourish, and adding these into the group mix provides greater leverage to bring talent into the light. In summarizing these three ingredients here, I remind you of the value of social proofing and accountability to the group. We behave differently when we know we are being observed, and in creating actions for optimizing collective talents I would urge you to use this aspect of human behaviour to your advantage.

1 Create tools and coaching methods that ignite the group's spirit of learning and curiosity.

We are born with a sense of curiosity and wonderment at the world around us. Everything is new and excites our keen interest to discover more. This is the spirit of learning required to tap the hidden depths of your talent potential and is typified by 'what if' language or 'tell me more' – the sense that everything is new, waiting yet to be discovered. When we 'grow up' we have that spirit of learning knocked out of us by the responses we experience to the questions we ask, and the spirit of discovery becomes jaded by the system so that we stop enquiring. The spirit of learning is also about stepping out of your comfort zone and knowing that someone will be around supporting you on your tentative first steps. Your role as the coach is to help create an environment in which it's ok not to be ok! By that I mean a 'safe' environment for your coachees to explore the extent of their comfort zones and then step out of them. Knowing that the group is there to help them navigate back to safety. Part of your coaching modus operandi is fostering wanton curiosity. Liberating talent starts with stepping out of the safety zone for the purpose of learning.

2 Create accountability within the group for the application of things that are learnt.

Moving out of your comfort zone is the first step – what you do with what you learn when 'outside the zone' is how you apply the learning. Talent remains dormant until and unless you apply the learning. This is typified by 'how do I do that? What do I need to do to improve? How can I improve? What do I need to practise?' In your coaching practice, if you are only asking your coachees to experience something once, they are missing out. Sometimes coachees will resist the application of learning because, guess what, it requires time, repetition, effort and a high degree of inspiration. Learning something new can be quite challenging so you have to feel inspired and want to learn in the first place to get you started. Without application, your coachees will experience a knowing–doing gap. Ironically, this can create a sense of failure over time as it becomes a point of frustration. Application is the state change from knowing to doing. Liberating talent can be like the birthing process. Lorna McDowell uses this metaphor to describe the effort really required for people to apply the lessons learned from the coaching. This is the point where the new-born is about to emerge and requires a final enormous effort for it to emerge into the light.

3 Create review mechanisms that encourage the group to persevere and reframe 'failures' as challenging and exciting learning points.

And so we move to the third ingredient necessary to liberate talent held in tension within your coachees – perseverance even in the face of tough feedback. When we learn something new we expect that part of the process will be trial and error. Yes, it helps to have someone show you the ropes, but only through your own exertions and experience can you truly understand what works for you. Human beings have the same basic design but each of us responds slightly differently to the same stimuli. This is why trial-and-error has to be experienced by the coachees directly so that they create muscle memory and thinking patterns, routines and habits that have meaning for them. Or course, you can role-model best practice *but* you don't know what the experience is like from inside the model system. You can only observe it, and in observing it you are processing it through your own experience. The final ingredient is shown in the commitment and willingness to act on feedback even when the going gets tough.

Developing your talents as a group coach

How should team coaches develop themselves? The first thing, it's not simple, it's not just that you can go and do a course and learn about it. You need to experience it too, integrate your existing wisdom and you need quite a few techniques from a range of disciplines as you journey towards mastery. You may have already got some of those tools but you need something to help bring them all altogether and integrate – therefore becoming a master group/team coach is about your own personal quest and discovery of the world and how it works. It is essential to learn in a group with other people and from the experience of those people.

- Development of meditation.

- Develop your body, movement, physical stamina. Your body as an organ, as a receiver.

- Somatic side of coaching.

- Spiritual awareness – awareness of what you do or don't believe. Separate from religion. An awareness of where anything comes from.

- Deep, deep ability to question – powerful questioning. Got to be curious about absolutely everything. So unless you have that desire, that fascination, to question why something is [sic].

- Supervision is essential both group and 1:1 essential. Capture your own learning. And any group coaching course – not a weekend course – should be a journey in itself. You've got to care about the world in order to put [aside] your own ego, to leave your own ego at the door.

Lorna McDowell, MD Xenergie

Optimizing collective talent requires 'systems thinking'

None of us exists in isolation from others, and our social needs mean that we enjoy and gain benefits from living in organized groups. This social aspect of our being human means that optimizing collective talents as an activity is not free from the system in which those latent talents have yet to be brought into existence. In other words, despite our best efforts, we can sometimes fall short of reaching our true potential because the system in which we live and work moderates our behaviour. When you coach people you are not coaching them in an isolated bubble – they interact with other people in their daily lives and live within different systems. We react, respond, interact and perform based on the complex interactions within the systems of which we are part. Making sense of these systems is about looking at the bigger picture and examining the feedback we are getting within that context. Sometimes coachees take actions that deliver surprising results – spending time assessing what might be happening in the system that delivered those results expands thinking and helps coachees see the world through different lenses. Exercises using perspectives and mapping help illuminate what might be happening within the system. Often we get caught up in the detail of what we do and in our ego-driven way see everything as being caused by our actions. The reality may be somewhat different. Take action to understand the system in which you are coaching your groups and be aware of when this system might be creating a barrier to talent emerging and developing.

Actions for optimizing collective talents are around creating tools, techniques and purpose around systemic change. The systemic change is both in the individual and in the way that individual's talents work in collaboration with other talents of people in the organization, their social systems and their business systems. If you look at leveraging talent on a global scale then it's about the economic and political systems as well – how can you leverage the latent talents? Optimizing talents in an 'organization' – ie a system – is about understanding that system and then doing something that will bring about positive change and make a difference in that system. There is something about the scale of group coaching, the fact that there are bigger numbers of people working together, that makes it possible to effect systemic change. And when that change is about creating a system to generate learning and bring out the latent talents of everyone in the organization, that can only be a good thing. Optimizing collective talents is an inclusive activity and one where talents are seen as abundant if you know where to look and how to nurture them.

Summary

My mission to tap into the total potential within organizations so that everyone has the opportunity to optimize their latent talent drives me, and in writing this book I hope I have shared some of the tools, techniques and the mindset that I endeavour to practise both in my work and in my social life. Helping others find their pot of gold talent is what defines me. Coaching for me is a means by which I can help other people liberate inherent talent and capability and I am at my best and I get my greatest buzz from working with people in groups. That collaborative spirit and really understanding what makes human beings so fascinating and full of potential is the real benefit of group coaching and that's what creates the buzz. It is humbling to be part of the group's development, observing people working together, learning together and improving together whilst having some amazing insights; experiencing groups optimizing their collective talents is the greatest joy of group coaching.

This book has hopefully given you some practical tools to work with your groups and food for thought as to why group coaching is a good thing to do, and challenged some of your thinking; if it's sparked in you an interest to find out more, mission accomplished! Whether you agree or don't agree with what I've written, the key thing is that it's catalysed your thinking, and ultimately coaching is about creating a system for thinking that then creates a system for learning, and through learning we develop our latent talents.

KEY POINTS FROM THE BOOK

- Being a group coach requires mental discipline and mastery in keeping your ego out of the process so that your coachees can find their own path to their talents.

- Working with groups has an inherent paradox in that the group looks to you for the process and at the same time seeks autonomy to explore topics on their own terms. Flexibility around your process is a fundamental prerequisite for group coaching to optimize talents.

- Let go of a need to use the 'right' tool and instead focus on the most useful tool to help the group move forward. Creativity is the start of developing a solutions mindset and helps your coachees ignite and generate a resourceful state of mind.

- Knowing where you want to end up is only part of the equation; just as important is knowing your starting point. Pay close attention to the system in which you are coaching people so that you and your coachees create realistic but challenging outcomes and review mechanisms, taking into account as many influencing factors as possible.

- We are all inherently capable of being talented. Inclusive strategies that see potential in everyone mean that you are leveraging each individual's innate resourcefulness. Finding a process or system that encompasses everyone within the organization is a sure-fire way to inspire reflection, engagement and activity. Tap into the benefits of using social activities to spark creativity and debate so that collective talent is optimized.

REFERENCES

Association for Coaching (nd) [online] http://www.associationforcoaching.com/pages/about/coaching-defined

Berne, Eric (1972) *What Do You Say After You Say Hello? The psychology of human destiny*, Grove Press, New York

Britton, Jennifer (2010) *Effective Group Coaching*, John Wiley & Sons, Mississauga, Ontario

Brown, Saul W, Grant, Anthony M (2010) From GROW to GROUP: theoretical issues and a practical model for group coaching in organisations, *Coaching: An international Journal of Theory, Research and Practice*, 3 (1), pp 30–45

Cialdini, Robert (2007) *Influence: The psychology of persuasion*, Collins Business Essentials, London

Cockerham, Ginger (2011) *Group Coaching: A comprehensive blueprint*, iUniverse.com

Doidge, Norman (2008) *The Brain That Changes Itself: Stories of personal triumph from the frontiers of brain science*, Penguin, London

Downey, Myles (2003) *Effective Coaching: Lessons from the coach's coach*, 3rd edn, Texerepublishing, San Francisco

Dweck, Carol S (2006) *Mindset: How you can fulfil your potential*, Ballantine Books Trade Paperback (Robinsons), New York

Dweck, Carol S (2012) The Right Mindset for Success, Harvard Business Review [online] http://blogs.hbr.org/ideacast/2012/01/the-right-mindset-for-success.html

Frankl, Viktor (1959) *Man's Search for Meaning*, Random House, New York

Gardner, Howard (1983) *Frames of Mind: The theory of multiple intelligences*, Basic Books, New York

Gorell, Ro (2011) *Are They On The Right Bus? The 55-minute guide to talent management*, Verb Publishing, Royston, UK

Hill, Napoleon (1937) *Think and Grow Rich*, The Ralston Society, Meridian, Conn

Jones, Gillian and Gorell, Ro (2012) *50 Top Tools For Coaching*, 2nd edn, Kogan Page, London

Karpman, Stephen B (nd) *Fairy Tales And Script Drama Analysis* [online] http://www.karpmandramatriangle.com/pdf/DramaTriangle.pdf

Krizman, J, Marian, V, Shook, A, Skoe, E and Kraus, N (2012) Sub cortical encoding of sound is enhanced in bilinguals and relates to executive function advantages, Proceedings of the National Academy of Sciences of the United States of America [online] www.pnas.org/cgi/doi/10.1073/pnas.1201575109

Lewin, K (1935) *A Dynamic Theory of Personality*, New York, McGraw-Hill

Luft, J and Ingham, H (1950) The Johari window: a graphic model of interpersonal awareness, *Proceedings of the Western Training Laboratory in Group Development*, UCLA, Los Angeles

McGovern, Joy, Lindemann, Michael, Vergara, Monica, Murphy, Stacey, Barker, Linda and Warrenfeltz, Rodney (2001) Maximising the impact of executive coaching: behavioural change, organisational outcomes and return on investment, *The Manchester Review*, 6 (1), pp 1–9

Pink, Daniel H (2011) *Drive: The surprising truth about what motivates us*, Canongate, Edinburgh

Rock, David (2009) *Your Brain at Work: Strategies for overcoming distraction, regaining focus and working all day long*, HarperCollins, New York

Schutz, William (1958) *FIRO: A three-dimensional theory of interpersonal behavior*, Holt, Rinehart, & Winston, New York

Senge, Peter M (2006) *The Fifth Discipline: The art and practice of the learning organisation*, 2nd edn, Random House Business Books, London

Shenk, David (2011) *The Genius in All of Us: Why everything you've been told about genetics, talent and intelligence is wrong*, Icom Books, London

Smith, Mark K (2001) Kurt Lewin: groups, experiential learning and action research [online] http://www.infed.org/thinkers/et-lewin.htm

Tuckman, BW (1965) Developmental sequence in small groups, *Psychological Bulletin*, 63 (6), pp 384–99

Young, JE (1999) Cognitive therapy for personality disorders: a schema-focused approach, Sarasota, Fl, Professional resource exchange, in *Transactional Analysis: An elegant theory and practice*, ed Claude Steiner [online] http://itaaworld.org/index.php/articles/26-6–transactional-analysis-an-elegant-theory-and-practice?showall=1&limitstart=

Zimbardo, Philip (2007) *The Lucifer Effect: Understanding how good people turn evil*, Random House, New York

Websites

The Association for Coaching: http://www.associationforcoaching.com

The world cafe: http://www.theworldcafe.com/

Will Schutz: http://thehumanelement.com/index.php/will-schutz

Process flow tools Smart Draw: http://www.smartdraw.com

Visio: http://visio.microsoft.com/en-us/preview/default.aspx

FURTHER READING

Bridges, William, (2004) *Managing Transitions: Making the most of change*, Da Capo Press, Cambridge, Mass

Ericsson, A K, Roring, Roy W and Nandagopal, Kiruthiga (June 2007) Giftedness and evidence for reproducibly superior performance: an account based on the expert performance framework, *High Ability Studies*, **18** (1) pp 3–56

Grint, Keith (December 2008) Wicked problems and clumsy solutions: the role of leadership, Clinical Leader, **1** (111), BAMM Publications [online] Webarchive.nationalarchives.gov.uk/20120810121037/ http://www.highways.gov.uk/business/documents/Keith_Grint_Wicked_ Problems_Clumsy_Solutions_presentation.pdf

Phillips, Christopher (2002) *Socrates Cafe: A fresh taste of philosophy*, WW Norton & Co, New York

Scharmer, Otto C (2009) *Theory U: Learning from the future as it emerges*, Berret-Koehler, San Francisco

Senge, Peter M, Jaworski, Joseph, Scharmer, Otto C and Flowers, Betty Sue (2005) Presence: *Exploring Profound Change in People, Organisations and Society*, Nicholas Brealey, London

Thibaut, John W, Kelley, Harold H (1959) *The Social Psychology of Groups*, John Wiley & Sons, New York

Useful websites

International Systemic Constellations Association: http://www.isca-network.org

International transactional analysis association: http://www.itaaworld.org

Website relating to Theory U and Otto Scharmer *et al*, work on presencing: http://www.presencing.com

Professor Philip Zimbardo's website. This includes material from the original Stanford Prison experiment: http://www.zimbardo.com

Xenergie: http://www.xenergie.com

The Clean Coaching Company: http://www.cleancoaching.com

INDEX

NB: page numbers in *italic* indicate figures or tables